Excel 2003:
Intermediate

Student Manual

Instructor - Joan Farouqi   10/11/07

THOMSON
™
COURSE TECHNOLOGY

Australia • Canada • Mexico • Singapore
Spain • United Kingdom • United States

Excel 2003: Intermediate

VP and GM of Courseware:	Michael Springer
Series Product Managers:	Adam A. Wilcox and Charles G. Blum
Developmental Editor:	Leslie Caico
Keytester:	Michele Jacobson
Series Designer:	Adam A. Wilcox
Cover Designer:	Abby Scholz

For more information contact:

Course Technology
25 Thomson Place
Boston, MA 02210

Or find us on the Web at: www.course.com

For permission to use material from this text or product, submit a request online at: www.thomsonrights.com

Any additional questions about permissions can be submitted by e-mail to: thomsonrights@thomson.com

Trademarks

Course ILT is a trademark of Course Technology.

Some of the product names and company names used in this book have been used for identification purposes only and may be trademarks or registered trademarks of their respective manufacturers and sellers.

Disclaimers

Course Technology reserves the right to revise this publication and make changes from time to time in its content without notice.

*The ProCert Labs numerical rating referenced is based on an independent review of this instructional material and is a separate analysis independent of Certiport or the Microsoft Office Specialist program.

Microsoft, the Office Logo, Excel, Outlook, and PowerPoint are either registered trademarks or trademarks of Microsoft Corporation in the United States and/or other countries. The Microsoft Office Specialist Logo is used under license from owner.

Certiport and the Certiport Approved Courseware logo are registered trademarks of Certiport Inc. in the United States and/or other countries.

Course Technology is independent from Microsoft Corporation or Certiport, and not affiliated with Microsoft or Certiport in any manner. While this publication may be used in assisting individuals to prepare for a Microsoft Office Specialist exam, Microsoft, Certiport, and Course Technology do not warrant that use of this publication will ensure passing a Microsoft Office Specialist exam.

ISBNs:

   ISBN-13: 978-1-4188-8934-0 = Student Manual
   ISBN-10: 1-4188-8934-2 = Student Manual

   ISBN-13: 978-1-4188-8936-4 = Student Manual with CDs (student data and CBT)
   ISBN-10: 1-4188-8936-9 = Student Manual with CDs (student data and CBT)

Printed in the United States of America

3 4 5 6 7 8 9 PM 08 07

What does the Microsoft® Office Specialist Approved Courseware logo represent?

Only the finest courseware receives approval to bear the Microsoft® Office Specialist logo. In order to give candidates the greatest chance of success at becoming a Microsoft Office Specialist, all approved courseware has been reviewed by an independent third party for quality of content and adherence to exam objectives. This specific course has been mapped to the following Microsoft Office Specialist Exam Skill Standards:

- Excel® 2003 Specialist
- Excel 2003 Expert

What is Microsoft Office Specialist certification?

Microsoft Office Specialist certification shows that employees, candidates and students have something exceptional to offer—proven expertise in Microsoft Office programs. Recognized by businesses and schools around the world, it is the only Microsoft-approved certification program of its kind. There are four levels of certification available: Specialist, Expert, Master, and Master Instructor.[1] Certification is available for the following Microsoft Office programs:

- Microsoft Word
- Microsoft Excel
- Microsoft Access
- Microsoft PowerPoint®
- Microsoft Outlook®
- Microsoft Project

For more information

To learn more about becoming a Microsoft Office Specialist, visit www.microsoft.com/officespecialist.

To learn about other Microsoft Office Specialist approved courseware from Course Technology, visit www.course.com.

---

[1]The availability of Microsoft Office Specialist certification exams varies by Microsoft Office program, program version, and language. Visit www.microsoft.com/officespecialist for exam availability.

Contents

Introduction

After reading this introduction, you will know how to:

A Use Course Technology ILT manuals in general.

B Use prerequisites, a target student description, course objectives, and a skills inventory to properly set your expectations for the course.

C Re-key this course after class.

Topic A: About the manual

Course Technology ILT philosophy

Course Technology ILT manuals facilitate your learning by providing structured interaction with the software itself. While we provide text to explain difficult concepts, the hands-on activities are the focus of our courses. By paying close attention as your instructor leads you through these activities, you will learn the skills and concepts effectively.

We believe strongly in the instructor-led classroom. During class, focus on your instructor. Our manuals are designed and written to facilitate your interaction with your instructor, and not to call attention to manuals themselves.

We believe in the basic approach of setting expectations, delivering instruction, and providing summary and review afterwards. For this reason, lessons begin with objectives and end with summaries. We also provide overall course objectives and a course summary to provide both an introduction to and closure on the entire course.

Manual components

The manuals contain these major components:

- Table of contents
- Introduction
- Units
- Appendices
- Course summary
- Quick reference
- Glossary
- Index

Each element is described below.

Table of contents

The table of contents acts as a learning roadmap.

Introduction

The introduction contains information about our training philosophy and our manual components, features, and conventions. It contains target student, prerequisite, objective, and setup information for the specific course.

Units

Units are the largest structural component of the course content. A unit begins with a title page that lists objectives for each major subdivision, or topic, within the unit. Within each topic, conceptual and explanatory information alternates with hands-on activities. Units conclude with a summary comprising one paragraph for each topic, and an independent practice activity that gives you an opportunity to practice the skills you've learned.

The conceptual information takes the form of text paragraphs, exhibits, lists, and tables. The activities are structured in two columns, one telling you what to do, the other providing explanations, descriptions, and graphics.

Appendices

An appendix is similar to a unit in that it contains objectives and conceptual explanations. However, an appendix does not include hands-on activities, a summary, or an independent practice activity. We have also included an appendix that lists all Microsoft Office Specialist exam objectives for Excel 2003 along with references to corresponding coverage in Course ILT courseware.

Course summary

This section provides a text summary of the entire course. It is useful for providing closure at the end of the course. The course summary also indicates the next course in this series, if there is one, and lists additional resources you might find useful as you continue to learn about the software.

Quick reference

The quick reference is an at-a-glance job aid summarizing some of the more common features of the software.

Glossary

The glossary provides definitions for all of the key terms used in this course.

Index

The index at the end of this manual makes it easy for you to find information about a particular software component, feature, or concept.

Manual conventions

We've tried to keep the number of elements and the types of formatting to a minimum in the manuals. This aids in clarity and makes the manuals more classically elegant looking. But there are some conventions and icons you should know about.

Convention	Description
Italic text	In conceptual text, indicates a new term or feature.
Bold text	In unit summaries, indicates a key term or concept. In an independent practice activity, indicates an explicit item that you select, choose, or type.
`Code font`	Indicates code or syntax.
`Longer strings of ▶ code will look ▶ like this.`	In the hands-on activities, any code that's too long to fit on a single line is divided into segments by one or more continuation characters (▶). This code should be entered as a continuous string of text.
Select **bold item**	In the left column of hands-on activities, bold sans-serif text indicates an explicit item that you select, choose, or type.
Keycaps like (↵ ENTER)	Indicate a key on the keyboard you must press.

Hands-on activities

The hands-on activities are the most important parts of our manuals. They are divided into two primary columns. The "Here's how" column gives short instructions to you about what to do. The "Here's why" column provides explanations, graphics, and clarifications. Here's a sample:

Do it!

A-1:   Creating a commission formula

Here's how	Here's why
1 Open Sales	This is an oversimplified sales compensation worksheet. It shows sales totals, commissions, and incentives for five sales reps.
2 Observe the contents of cell F4	F4 ▼ = =E4*C_Rate The commission rate formulas use the name "C_Rate" instead of a value for the commission rate.

For these activities, we have provided a collection of data files designed to help you learn each skill in a real-world business context. As you work through the activities, you will modify and update these files. Of course, you might make a mistake and, therefore, want to re-key the activity starting from scratch. To make it easy to start over, you will rename each data file at the end of the first activity in which the file is modified. Our convention for renaming files is to add the word "My" to the beginning of the file name. In the above activity, for example, a file called "Sales" is being used for the first time. At the end of this activity, you would save the file as "My sales," thus leaving the "Sales" file unchanged. If you make a mistake, you can start over using the original "Sales" file.

In some activities, however, it may not be practical to rename the data file. If you want to retry one of these activities, ask your instructor for a fresh copy of the original data file.

Topic B: Setting your expectations

Properly setting your expectations is essential to your success. This topic will help you do that by providing:

- Prerequisites for this course
- A description of the target student at whom the course is aimed
- A list of the objectives for the course
- A skills assessment for the course

Course prerequisites

Before taking this course, you should be familiar with personal computers and the use of a keyboard and a mouse. Furthermore, this course assumes that you've completed the following courses or have equivalent experience:

- *Windows 2000: Basic*
- *Excel 2003: Basic*

Target student

Before taking this course, you should be comfortable using a personal computer and Microsoft Windows 98 or later. You should have some experience using Microsoft Excel. You will get the most out of this course if your goal is to become proficient in using such Excel features as customizing toolbars and menus, consolidating data, using advanced chart formatting options, sorting and filtering lists, using special formatting options, using templates, using error tracing features, protecting worksheets, and linking worksheets by using 3-D formulas.

Microsoft Office Specialist certification

This course is designed to help you pass both Microsoft Office Specialist exams for Excel 2003 (Specialist and Expert). For complete certification training, you should complete this course as well as:

- *Excel 2003: Basic*
- *Excel 2003: Advanced*

Course objectives

These overall course objectives will give you an idea about what to expect from the course. It is also possible that they will help you see that this course is not the right one for you. If you think you either lack the prerequisite knowledge or already know most of the subject matter to be covered, you should let your instructor know that you think you are misplaced in the class.

Note: In addition to the general objectives listed below, specific Microsoft Office Specialist exam objectives are listed at the beginning of each topic. For a complete mapping of exam objectives to Course ILT content, see Appendix B.

After completing this course, you will know how to:

- Navigate large worksheets effectively by using magnification, frozen panes, and split panes; and control the printing of large worksheets.
- Navigate, manage, and print multiple worksheets; link workbooks by using 3-D formulas; and summarize data by using the Consolidate command.
- Change the View, General, and Calculation settings of Excel; and customize toolbars and menus.
- Add borders and shading; apply special formats; create, apply, and modify styles; and change the orientation of cells.
- Sort lists by columns; and filter lists based on complex criteria.
- Format data points; create combination charts and trendlines; and add and format graphic elements.
- Use auditing features; add comments and text boxes; and protect a worksheet or part of a worksheet.
- Work with Excel's built-in templates; and create and manage custom templates.

Skills inventory

Use the following form to gauge your skill level entering the class. For each skill listed, rate your familiarity from 1 to 5, with five being the most familiar. *This is not a test.* Rather, it is intended to provide you with an idea of where you're starting from at the beginning of class. If you're wholly unfamiliar with all the skills, you might not be ready for the class. If you think you already understand all of the skills, you might need to move on to the next course in the series. In either case, you should let your instructor know as soon as possible.

Skill	1	2	3	4	5
Zooming in and out on a large worksheet					
Freezing and unfreezing panes					
Hiding and unhiding data, and creating outlines					
Setting print titles and page breaks, and using Page Break Preview					
Navigating, managing, and printing multiple worksheets					
Creating 3-D formulas to link worksheets and workbooks					
Adding a Watch window					
Using the Consolidate command to summarize data					
Linking workbooks, creating external links, and redirecting links					
Changing View, General, and Calculation settings					
Customizing toolbars and menus					
Adding borders and shading to cells					
Applying number, date, and time formats					
Creating, modifying, and applying styles					
Merging and splitting cells, and changing cell orientation					
Sorting and filtering lists					
Using advanced filtering options					
Using advanced chart formatting options					

Skill	1	2	3	4	5
Creating combination charts and trendlines					
Inserting and formatting graphic elements					
Using auditing features					
Adding comments and text boxes					
Protecting a worksheet					
Using built-in templates, and creating and managing templates					

Topic C: Re-keying the course

If you have the proper hardware and software, you can re-key this course after class. This section explains what you'll need in order to do so, and how to do it.

Computer requirements

To re-key this course, your personal computer must have:

- A keyboard and a mouse
- Pentium 233 MHz processor (or higher)
- At least 128 MB RAM
- At least 400 MB of available hard drive space
- CD-ROM drive
- SVGA monitor (800×600 minimum resolution support)
- A printer driver (An actual printer is not required, but you will not be able to use the Page Break Preview feature in Unit 1 unless a driver is installed.)
- Internet access, if you want to download the Student Data files from www.courseilt.com, and for downloading the latest updates and service packs from www.windowsupdate.com

Setup instructions to re-key the course

Before you re-key the course, you will need to perform the following steps.

1   Install Microsoft Windows 2000 Professional on an NTFS partition according to the software manufacturer's instructions. Then, install the latest critical updates and service packs from www.windowsupdate.com. (You can also use Windows XP Professional, although the screen shots in this course were taken using Windows 2000, so your screens might look somewhat different.)

2   Adjust your computer's display properties as follows:

   a   Open the Control Panel and double-click Display to open the Display Properties dialog box.

   b   On the Settings tab, change the Colors setting to True Color (24 bit or 32 bit) and the Screen area to 800 by 600 pixels.

   c   On the Appearance tab, set the Scheme to Windows Classic.

   d   Click OK. If you are prompted to accept the new settings, click OK and click Yes. Then, if necessary, close the Display Properties dialog box.

3   Adjust your computer's Internet settings as follows:

   a   On the desktop, right-click the Internet Explorer icon and choose Properties to open the Internet Properties dialog box.

   b   On the Connections tab, click Setup to start the Internet Connection Wizard.

   c   Click Cancel. A message box will appear.

   d   Check "Do not show the Internet Connection wizard in the future" and click Yes.

   e   Re-open the Internet Properties dialog box.

   f   On the General tab, click Use Blank, click Apply, and click OK.

4 If your computer is connected to a printer, install the appropriate drivers. If your computer is not connected to a printer, install a printer driver of your choice. (If a printer was connected to the computer during the installation of Windows, there will be a driver installed for that printer. If not, you should install a standard PostScript printer driver, such as HP LaserJet 5.)

5 Install Microsoft Office 2003 according to the software manufacturer's instructions, as follows:

  a When prompted for the CD key, enter the 25-character code included with your software.

  b Select the Custom installation option and click Next.

  c Clear all check boxes except Microsoft Excel.

  d Select "Choose advanced customization of applications" and click Next.

  e Next to Microsoft Office Excel for Windows, click the drop-down arrow and choose Run all from My Computer.

  f Next to Office Shared Features, click the drop-down arrow and choose Run all from My Computer.

  g Click Next. Then, click Install to start the installation.

  h When the installation has completed successfully, click Finish.

6 If necessary, download the Student Data files for the course. (If you don't have an Internet connection, you can ask your instructor for a copy of the data files on a disk.)

  a Connect to www.courseilt.com/instructor_tools.html.

  b Click the link for Microsoft Excel 2003 to display a page of course listings, and then click the link for Excel 2003: Intermediate, 2nd Edition.

  c Click the link for downloading the Student Data files, and follow the instructions that appear on your screen.

7 Copy the data files to the Student Data folder.

8 Configure Windows Explorer to show hidden files and folders.

  a Start Windows Explorer.

  b Choose Tools, Folder Options, and then activate the View tab.

  c Under Advanced settings, select "Show hidden files and folders."

  d Click OK and then close Windows Explorer.

9 Start Excel. Then, turn off the Office Assistant, as follows:

  a If the Office Assistant is not displayed, choose Help, Show the Office Assistant.

  b Right-click the Office Assistant and choose Options to open the Office Assistant dialog box.

  c Clear Use the Office Assistant and click OK.

10 Dock the Formatting toolbar below the Standard toolbar.

11 Hide the Language Bar. To do so:

  a Click Start and choose Settings, Control Panel.

  b Double-click Text Services to open the Text Services dialog box.

  c Under Preference, click the Language Bar button to open the Language Bar settings dialog box.

  d Clear Show the language bar on the desktop.

  e Click OK.

12 Display the Borders toolbar, and then dock it below the Formatting toolbar.

13 Close any open task panes. To close the Startup task pane:

   a Choose Tools, Options to open the Options dialog box.

   b Activate the View tab.

   c Clear Startup Task Pane

   d Click OK.

14 Set Excel's default file location to C:\Student Data, as follows:

   a Choose Tools, Options to open the Options dialog box.

   b Activate the General tab.

   c In the Default file location box, enter C:\Student Data.

   d Click OK.

15 Close Excel.

CertBlaster test preparation for Microsoft Office Specialist certification

If you are interested in attaining Microsoft Office Specialist certification, you can download CertBlaster test preparation software for Excel 2003 from the Course ILT Web site. Here's what you do:

1 Go to www.courseilt.com/certblaster.

2 Click the link for Excel 2003.

3 Save the .EXE file to a folder on your hard drive. (**Note**: If you skip this step, the CertBlaster software will not install correctly.)

4 Click Start and choose Run.

5 Click Browse and then navigate to the folder that contains the .EXE file.

6 Select the .EXE file and click Open.

7 Click OK and follow the on-screen instructions. When prompted for the password, enter **c_excel**.

Unit 1

Working with large worksheets

Freezing panes

Outlining –
Data –
group & outline
Select items
to outline
auto out-
line
group line

reverse under selection
go back and deselect
ungroup.

Unit time: 30 minutes

Complete this unit, and you'll know how to:

A Zoom in and out of a large worksheet, use the Freeze Panes command, and split a worksheet.

B Hide and display data, and create outlines to organize data.

C Set print titles and set page breaks by using the Insert command and the Page Break Preview feature.

Topic A: Viewing options

This topic covers the following Microsoft Office Specialist exam objective.

#	Objective
XL03S-5-6	Splitting, freezing/unfreezing, arranging and hiding/unhiding workbooks (This objective is also covered in Topic B and in the unit titled "Using multiple worksheets and workbooks.")

Zooming in and out

Explanation

To increase or decrease the visible area of a worksheet, you can use the Zoom command. To do this:

1 Choose View, Zoom to open the Zoom dialog box.

2 Under Magnification, select a magnification percentage. A higher percentage will show less of the worksheet, and a lower percentage will show more.

3 Click OK.

You can also specify the magnification percentage in the Zoom box on the Standard toolbar, as shown in Exhibit 1-1.

Zoom box

Exhibit 1-1: The Zoom box on the Standard toolbar

Do it!   **A-1:   Zooming in and out on a large worksheet**

Here's how	Here's why
1 Start Excel	Click Start, and choose Programs, Microsoft Office, Microsoft Office Excel 2003.
2 Open Large worksheet	(From the current unit folder.) This worksheet contains quarterly sales of different products for the years 2000–2005. You'll zoom in and out on this worksheet to view more or less of the data.
3 Save the workbook as **My large worksheet**	In the current unit folder.
4 Choose **View**, **Zoom...**	To open the Zoom dialog box. Notice that 100% is selected by default.
Under Magnification, select **50%**	
Click **OK**	The value in the Zoom box changes to 50%. You can now view more cells on screen, although it might be difficult to read the data.
5 Click as shown	50%
	Notice that the Zoom list displays several magnification values.
Select **100%**	To magnify the worksheet area to its default size.

Freezing panes

Explanation

When you work with a large worksheet, not all the data will be visible at the same time. You can use the Freeze Panes command to lock row or column headings in place so that when you scroll, these headings will remain visible.

You can freeze selected data in the following ways:

- For freezing a row, select the row below the row to be frozen, and choose Window, Freeze Panes.

- For freezing a column, select the column to the right of the column to be frozen, and choose Window, Freeze Panes.

- For freezing a specific row and column, select a cell below and to the right of the headings to be frozen, and choose Window, Freeze Panes.

To unfreeze panes, choose Window, Unfreeze Panes.

Do it!

A-2:   Using the Freeze Panes command

Here's how	Here's why
1 Scroll the worksheet horizontally and vertically	As you scroll horizontally, the product names are not visible. When you scroll vertically, the headings are not visible. To view these headings and names, you can freeze the panes.
2 Select B6	To freeze row and column headings, you begin by selecting a cell below and to the right of the headings you want to freeze. By selecting B6, you'll freeze the heading in rows 1 through 5, as well as column A.
3 Choose **Window, Freeze Panes**	To freeze the selected panes.
4 Scroll the worksheet horizontally	To view the data in the other columns. The data in the Product column remains visible as you scroll horizontally.
5 Scroll the worksheet vertically	To view the data in the other rows. The column headings remain visible as you scroll down.
6 Choose **Window, Unfreeze Panes**	To unfreeze the frozen group of cells.

Splitting a worksheet into panes

Explanation

When using large worksheets, you might need to work with sets of data in distant locations on the sheet. By splitting a worksheet into panes, you can view different areas simultaneously. Unlike freezing panes, when you split a window, you can navigate in each pane.

You can split a worksheet horizontally, vertically, or both.

- To split a worksheet horizontally, point to the *split box* at the top of the vertical scroll bar, shown in Exhibit 1-2. The mouse pointer changes to a *split pointer* shape, shown in Exhibit 1-3. Drag the split box down to the position where you would like to split the screen.

- To split a worksheet vertically, point to the split box to the left of the horizontal scroll bar. The mouse pointer changes to a split pointer shape. Drag the split box to the left to the position where you would like to split the screen.

Exhibit 1-2: The split box

Exhibit 1-3: The split pointer

To return the split box to its original location, simply double-click it. Your worksheet will then return to a single pane.

Do it!

A-3:   Splitting a worksheet into panes

Here's how	Here's why
1 Place the mouse pointer over the split box	(The split box is located at the top of the vertical scroll bar.) The mouse pointer changes to a split pointer shape.
2 Drag down to row 12	To split the display screen into two panes.
3 Scroll the top pane	You can navigate to any location you like.
4 Scroll the bottom pane	You can navigate independently from the top pane.
5 Double-click the split box	(Located in the vertical scroll bar where the two panes are split.) To return the split box to its original location and return the worksheet to a single pane.

Topic B: Hiding, displaying, and outlining data

This topic covers the following Microsoft Office Specialist exam objectives.

#	Objective
XL03S-3-3	Inserting and deleting, hiding and unhiding rows and columns (This objective is also covered in the Excel 2003: Basic course in the unit titled "Modifying a worksheet.")
XL03S-3-4	Hiding and unhiding worksheets
XL03E-1-3	Grouping and outlining data

The Hide and Unhide commands

Explanation

You can hide a row or column by selecting it and using the Format menu. For example, to hide a column, select the column and choose Format, Column, Hide. Exhibit 1-4 displays a worksheet in which the columns containing quarterly sales details are hidden. It shows only the Total columns for the five years 2000–2005. The Total column for 2000–2001 (column F) appears immediately after the Product column (column A). The columns in between (B through E) are hidden. Although they have not been deleted, you cannot see them.

You'll need to unhide hidden rows and columns when you want to use or view them again. To unhide rows, select the rows on either side of the hidden row(s), and choose Format, Row, Unhide. To unhide columns, select the columns on either side of the hidden column(s), and choose Format, Column, Unhide.

Similarly, you can hide an entire worksheet by selecting that sheet's tab and choosing Format, Sheet, Hide. You can unhide the sheet by choosing Format, Sheet, Unhide. The Unhide dialog box will appear with all hidden sheets listed. Select the sheet you would like to unhide, and click OK.

	A	F	K	P	U	Z
1	**Outlander Spices**					
2	**Quarterly sales 2000 - 2005**					
3						
4		**2000-2001**	**2001-2002**	**2002-2003**	**2003-2004**	**2004-2005**
5	**Product**	**Total**	**Total**	**Total**	**Total**	**Total**
6	Dill Seed	$23,442	$20,345	$29,196	$35,902	$23,442
7	Mustard Seed	$24,755	$26,400	$34,879	$41,886	$24,755
8	Coriander Powder	$23,765	$29,688	$28,689	$36,485	$23,765
9	Turmeric	$23,831	$23,055	$37,545	$36,461	$23,831
10	Cinnamon (Ground Korintje)	$26,466	$33,404	$19,761	$41,993	$26,466
11	Cinnamon (Ground) Extra High Oil (2X)	$1,845	$2,253	$2,139	$2,644	$1,845
12	Cinnamon (Ground) High Oil (1X)	$1,753	$2,146	$1,871	$2,819	$1,753

Exhibit 1-4: A sales worksheet with quarterly sales columns hidden

Do it!

B-1:   Hiding and unhiding columns and worksheets

Here's how	Here's why
1 Select columns B:E	
2 Choose **Format**, **Column**, **Hide**	To hide the quarterly sales details and display only the total sales for the year 2000–2001.
3 Hide the quarterly sales details for the remaining years	(Select the columns you want to hide, and choose Format, Column, Hide.) To display only the total sales columns for the five years, as shown in Exhibit 1-4.
4 Select columns A:F	To unhide columns B:E, you must select the columns surrounding them.
5 Choose **Format**, **Column**, **Unhide**	To unhide columns B:E. The worksheet now displays the quarterly sales details for 2000–2001.
6 Unhide the remaining hidden columns	(Select columns F:Z, and choose Format, Column, Unhide.)
7 Click the Product details sheet tab	To select the sheet.
8 Choose **Format**, **Sheet**, **Hide**	The Product details sheet is no longer visible.
9 Choose **Format**, **Sheet**, **Unhide...**	The Product details sheet is selected as the only sheet currently hidden in this workbook.
Click **OK**	To unhide the sheet.
10 Update the workbook	

Outlines

Explanation

You can organize data in a worksheet by creating an outline. An outline groups data by levels. Each level contains a section of the data that you can expand or collapse. A worksheet can have up to eight levels of detail.

To outline data:

1 Select the range of cells for which you want to create an outline.
2 Verify that the summary rows or columns you want to outline are located in the same position relative to the detailed data. For example, the summary columns might be located either to the right or to the left of the detailed data, but not in both positions.
3 Choose Data, Group and Outline, Auto Outline.

After creating an outline, you can use the outline symbols to expand and collapse data, as shown in Exhibit 1-5 and Exhibit 1-6. You can also expand or collapse data by row or column level. You can click the highest-level button to show all details, and click the lowest-level button to hide all details. For example, if an outline has four levels, click 4 to show details of all four levels, and click 1 to hide all details.

Selecting a large range

When using a large worksheet, you might need to select a range that covers several screens. It can be difficult to select this range by dragging. Another way to select such a range is to click the first cell in the range, press and hold Shift, and click the last cell in the range.

Row-level symbols   Column-level symbols   Collapse symbol

	A	B	C	D	E	F	G
					2000-2001		
1	**Outlander Spices**						
2	**Quarterly sales 2000 - 2005**						
3							
4					2000-2001		
5	Product	Qtr1	Qtr2	Qtr3	Qtr4	Total	Qtr1
6	Dill Seed	$6,354	$4,846	$3,958	$8,284	$23,442	$5,235
7	Mustard Seed	$8,484	$5,858	$5,858	$4,555	$24,755	$9,041
8	Coriander Powder	$9,595	$5,859	$4,879	$3,432	$23,765	$10,243
9	Turmeric	$7,578	$6,900	$3,444	$5,909	$23,831	$8,457
10	Cinnamon (Ground Korintje)	$6,291	$5,209	$6,333	$8,633	$26,466	$9,457
11	Cinnamon (Ground) Extra High Oil (2X)	$791	$278	$298	$478	$1,845	$734
12	Cinnamon (Ground) High Oil (1X)	$432	$322	$245	$754	$1,753	$436
13	Angelica Root	$6,354	$6,563	$4,333	$8,284	$25,534	$3,466

Exhibit 1-5: The expanded form

Lowest-level buttons   Highest-level buttons   Expand symbol

	A	F	K	P
1	**Outlander Spices**			
2	**Quarterly sales 2000 - 2005**			
3				
4		**2000-2001**	**2001-2002**	**2002-2003**
5	**Product**	**Total**	**Total**	**Total**
41	**Total**	$345,773	$410,060	$402,127

Exhibit 1-6: The collapsed form

Do it!

B-2:   Creating an outline

Here's how	Here's why
1 In the Quarterly sales sheet, select A6	If necessary, click the Quarterly sales tab to move to the Quarterly sales worksheet.
Press and hold (SHIFT) and select Z41	To select the range A6:Z41
Release (SHIFT)	
2 Choose **Data**, **Group and Outline**, **Auto Outline**	To outline the selected data. Various symbols appear above and to the left of the worksheet.
3 Click the collapse symbol above column F	

	A	F	G
1	**Outlander Spices**		
2	**Quarterly sales 2000 - 2005**		
3			
4		**2000-2001**	
5	**Product**	**Total**	**Qtr1**
6	Dill Seed	$23,442	$5,235
7	Mustard Seed	$24,755	$9,041
8	Coriander Powder	$23,785	$10,243

(The collapse symbol resembles a minus sign.) To collapse the quarterly sales data of 2000-2001 and show only the total sales. There is now an expand symbol (+) above column F. The quarterly sales data for the years 2001 to 2005 is still visible.

4 Collapse the quarterly sales data for the years 2001 to 2005	

		A	F	K
1		**Outlander Spices**		
2		**Quarterly sales 2000 - 2005**		
3				
4			2000-2001	2001-2002
5		Product	Total	Total
6		Dill Seed	$23,442	$20,345
7		Mustard Seed	$24,755	$26,400
8		Coriander Powder	$23,765	$29,699

(Click the collapse symbols above columns K, P, U, and Z.) To display only the total sales data for the years 2000 to 2005. Expand symbols now appear above the five visible columns.

5 Click the expand symbol above column F	The quarterly sales data for 2000–2001 appears, and there is now a collapse symbol above column F.
6 Click the column-level symbol **2**	To expand the remaining collapsed column data.
7 Click the row-level symbol **1**	To collapse the row-level data. Detailed data of quarterly sales by product for each year disappears, and only the overall total of quarterly sales for each year is visible.
8 Click the row-level symbol **2**	To expand the row-level data. It displays the detailed data for the years 2000 to 2005.
9 Choose **Data**, **Group and Outline**, **Clear Outline**	To clear the outlines.
10 Update the workbook	

Topic C: Printing large worksheets

This topic covers the following Microsoft Office Specialist exam objectives.

#	Objective
XL03S-5-5	Previewing page breaks
XL03S-5-7	Viewing and modifying page breaks

Print titles

Explanation

When you need to print a large worksheet, first preview it to see how it will appear when printed. You'll notice that the titles of the worksheets appear on only the first page. This makes the data on the other pages hard to interpret. You can set *print titles* for the text that you want to print as headings on all the pages.

To set print titles:

1 Choose View, Header and Footer to open the Page Setup dialog box.
2 Activate the Sheet tab. Under Print titles, enter the range of the titles that you want to print on each page. You can select the rows to repeat at the top of all the pages, columns to repeat at the left of all the pages, or both.
3 Click OK.

Do it! **C-1: Setting print titles**

Here's how	Here's why
1 Click	(The Print Preview button is on the Standard toolbar.) To preview the worksheet to see how it would look when printed.
Click **Zoom**	To view the data clearly.
Click **Next**	To move to the next page in the preview. The data on this page doesn't have row titles and is difficult to interpret. You'll add print titles to all the pages.
2 Click **Close**	Automatic page breaks appear as dashed lines to the left of columns F, N, and V.
3 Choose **View, Header and Footer...**	To open the Page Setup dialog box. Notice that the Header/Footer tab is activated by default.
Click the **Sheet** tab	
Click as shown	
	To collapse the Page Setup dialog box. The title bar of the dialog box shows Page Setup – Columns to repeat at left:. You'll set product names, the company name, and the subtitle as print titles so that they appear on every page.
4 Click column A	To select the entire column.
Click	(The Collapse Dialog button is in the Page Setup dialog box.) To expand the Page Setup dialog box. The selected range appears in the Columns to repeat at left box.
5 Click **Print Preview**	To see a preview of the worksheet. The first page has relevant print titles.
Click **Next**	The print titles that you set now appear on every page. However, with the existing automatic page breaks, data for the individual years spills over from page to page.
6 Click **Close**	Now the automatic page breaks appear to the left of columns F, J, N, R, V, and Z.
7 Update the workbook	

Page breaks

Explanation

Excel inserts automatic page breaks that appear as dashed lines in a worksheet. These page break lines help you see how the data will be divided among the printed pages. Sometimes, data that should appear together will fall on separate pages. To change this, you can insert manual page breaks, which appear as solid lines in a worksheet.

To insert a vertical page break, select the column to the left of where you want to place the page break, and choose Insert, Page Break. To insert a horizontal page break, select the row above where you want to insert the page break, and choose Insert, Page Break.

Do it!

C-2:   Setting page breaks

Here's how	Here's why
1 Click column G	To select the entire column. You'll insert a page break to the left of column G so that all data for 2000–2001 appears on the same page.
2 Choose **Insert**, **Page Break**	
Deselect the cells	A manual page break appears as a solid line to the left of column G.
3 Set a manual page break to the left of column L	(Click column L, and choose Insert, Page Break.)
Set manual page breaks to the left of columns Q and V	
4 Update the workbook	

Page Break Preview

Explanation

You can use the Page Break Preview command to see where page breaks will occur when a worksheet is printed. If you don't like the placement of the page breaks, you can drag them to a new position in Page Break Preview.

To preview page breaks, choose View, Page Break Preview. In Page Break Preview, manually inserted page breaks appear as solid blue lines, and automatically inserted page breaks appear as dashed blue lines, as shown in Exhibit 1-7.

	A	B	C	D	E	F	G	H	I	J	K	L
1	**Outlander Spices**											
2	Quarterly sales 2000 - 2005											
3												
4				2000-2001					2001-2002			
5	Product	Qtr1	Qtr2	Qtr3	Qtr4	Total	Qtr1	Qtr2	Qtr3	Qtr4	Total	Qtr1
6	Dill Seed	$6,354	$4,846	$3,958	$8,284	$23,442	$5,235	$6,333	$2,535	$6,242	$20,345	$8,990
7	Mustard Seed	$8,484	$5,858	$5,858	$4,555	$24,755	$9,041	$8,364	$6,349	$2,646	$26,400	$8,926
8	Coriander Powder	$9,595	$5,859	$4,879	$3,432	$23,765	$10,243	$8,925	$5,254	$5,266	$29,688	$9,827
9	Turmeric	$7,578	$6,900	$3,444	$5,909	$23,831	$8,457	$2,466	$7,466	$4,666	$23,055	$8,922
10	Cinnamon (Ground Korintje)	$6,291	$5,209	$6,333	$8,633	$26,466	$9,457	$7,457	$7,545	$8,945	$33,404	$2,266
11	Cinnamon (Ground) Extra High Oil (2	$791	$278	$298	$478	$1,845	$734	$642	$345	$532	$2,253	$634
12	Cinnamon (Ground) High Oil (1X)	$432	$322	$245	$754	$1,753	$436	$733	$634	$343	$2,146	$343
13	Angelica Root	$6,354	$6,563	$4,333	$8,284	$25,534	$3,466	$2,662	$6,422	$6,222	$18,772	$4,632
14	Anise	$789	$434	$564	$633	$2,420	$422	$624	$733	$732	$2,511	$574
15	Anise Seeds	$534	$423	$521	$625	$2,103	$833	$733	$1,065	$1,198	$3,829	$734
16	Annatto Seed	$644	$643	$634	$632	$2,553	$636	$732	$477	$845	$2,690	$856
17	Asafoetida Powder	$654	$634	$326	$754	$2,368	$753	$844	$1,024	$1,157	$3,778	$688
18	Basil Leaf (Whole)	$6,778	$6,760	$4,568	$7,834	$25,940	$8,566	$9,556	$8,554	$7,886	$34,562	$9,555
19	Basil Leaf (Ground)	$6,354	$6,346	$3,555	$6,442	$22,697	$7,464	$8,444	$5,858	$8,445	$30,211	$7,866
20	Bay Leaf (Whole)	$283	$532	$525	$652	$1,942	$577	$855	$944	$734	$3,010	$667
21	Bay Leaf (Ground)	$543	$634	$744	$543	$2,464	$733	$742	$983	$732	$3,190	$595

Exhibit 1-7: Page Break Preview

Do it!

C-3:   Using Page Break Preview

Here's how	Here's why
1 Choose **View**, **Page Break Preview**	To open the Welcome to Page Break Preview message box. You'll view the page breaks for this worksheet and set manual page breaks by dragging the page breaks to new locations.
2 Check **Do not show this dialog again.**	To ensure that when you open subsequent worksheets by using Page Break Preview, this message box does not appear again.
Click **OK**	To close the message box. Solid and dashed blue lines, indicating manual and automatic page breaks, respectively, appear on the worksheet. The page numbers also appear in the background. You'll set a manual page break after each year's Total column by dragging the automatic page breaks. The first automatic page break is visible as a dashed blue line before the Total column of 2000–2001.
3 Point to the first automatic-page-break line	(The page break line is between columns E and F.) The shape of the pointer changes to a double-headed arrow.
Drag the pointer to the right edge of column F	To move the page-break line, inserting only a manual page break after column F. The page-break line now appears as a solid blue line between columns F and G. Now, all data for 2000–2001 appears together on the same page.
Observe the next page break	The manual page break that was before column K has disappeared. This occurred because when you move one page break, the other page breaks are automatically moved. This changes the scaling of the entire sheet, and you can fit more columns on a page.
4 Preview the worksheet	(Click the Print Preview button on the Standard toolbar.) Data for 2000–2001 appears together on the same page.
Preview the other pages	(Click the Next button.) Now, all the pages have relevant print titles. In addition, related data appears together on the same page.
Click **Close**	
5 Update and close the workbook	

Unit summary: Working with large worksheets

Topic A In this topic, you learned how to **zoom in** and **zoom out** on a large worksheet to view more or less of the data. You also learned how to **freeze panes** to keep selected row or column headings and groups of cells in place as you scroll through the worksheet. Then, you learned how to **split panes** to access two distant worksheet locations simultaneously.

Topic B In this topic, you learned how to **hide** and **unhide** columns and worksheets to display only the data you need. You also learned how to create an **outline** to summarize data by levels.

Topic C In this topic, you learned how to set **print titles** so that headings appear on every page. In addition, you learned how to set **page breaks** by using the **Insert**, **Page Break** command. You also used the **Page Break Preview** feature to view and adjust page breaks.

Independent practice activity

1 Open Practice sales data (from the current unit folder), and save it as **My practice sales data**.

2 Freeze all the information in column A and rows 1 through 4. Scroll vertically and horizontally, and then unfreeze the information.

3 Hide all columns except Product, Region, Total purchase, Total sale, and Total value of stock.

4 Unhide all the hidden columns.

5 If necessary, scroll vertically and horizontally to view all the rows and columns.

6 Create an outline on the worksheet. (*Hint:* Select A5:J43.)

7 Compare your worksheet with Exhibit 1-8.

8 Experiment with all the outline symbols. Then, show all detail.

9 Set print titles so that the company name, subtitle, product names, and region names appear on every page.

10 Use Page Break Preview to adjust the page breaks so that data appears on two pages.

11 Preview and zoom in on the worksheet.

12 Compare the preview of the second page with Exhibit 1-9.

13 Update and close the workbook.

	Product	Region	Units purchased	Cost per unit	Total purchase	Units sold
1	**Outlander Spices**					
2	Purchase/sales report 2000-2005					
3						
4	Product	Region	Units purchased	Cost per unit	Total purchase	Units sold
5	Cinnamon (Ground Korintje)	East	$1,632	$20	$32,640	$1,600
6	Cinnamon (Ground) Extra High Oil (2X)	East	$1,730	$22	$38,060	$1,650
7	Cinnamon (Ground) High Oil (1X)	East	$1,239	$34	$42,126	$1,100
8	Angelica Root	East	$1,709	$34	$58,106	$1,500
9	Anise	East	$1,429	$45	$64,305	$1,345
10	Anise Seeds	East	$1,499	$53	$79,447	$1,311
11	Annatto Speed	East	$1,984	$23	$45,632	$1,789
12	Asafoetida Powder	East	$1,046	$13	$13,598	$690
13	**Sub Total(East)**		$12,268		$373,914	$10,985

Exhibit 1-8: A sample of the My practice sales data workbook after step 6

Outlander Spices
Purchase/sales report 2000-2005

Product	Region	Selling price per unit	Total sale	Units on hand	Total value of stock
Cinnamon (Ground Korintje)	East	$60	$80,000	$32	$640
Cinnamon (Ground) Extra High Oil (2X)	East	$35	$57,750	$80	$1,760
Cinnamon (Ground) High Oil (1X)	East	$40	$44,000	$139	$4,726
Angelica Root	East	$65	$97,500	$209	$7,106
Anise	East	$60	$80,700	$84	$3,780
Anise Seeds	East	$70	$91,770	$188	$9,964
Annatto Speed	East	$50	$89,450	$195	$4,485
Asafoetida Powder	East	$33	$22,770	$356	$4,628
Sub Total(East)			$563,940	$1,283	$37,089
Basil Leaf (Whole)	North	$125	$250,000	$1,904	$156,128
Basil Leaf (Ground)	North	$96	$48,000	$1,494	$62,748
Bay Leaf (Whole)	North	$35	$245,000	$1,984	$23,808
Bay Leaf (Ground)	North	$45	$292,500	$3,500	$122,500
Caraway Seed (Whole)	North	$25	$28,475	$620	$10,540
Caraway Seed (Ground)	North	$30	$160,230	$2,142	$57,834
Cardamom Seed (Whole)	North	$30	$223,360	$6,729	$174,954
Cardamom Seed (Ground)	North	$25	$168,075	$2,060	$39,140
Carob Powder (Raw)	North	$27	$213,921	$1,388	$31,924
Carob Pods (Ribbled)	North	$35	$31,500	$960	$30,720
Sub Total(North)			$1,666,061	$3,687,162	$710,296

Exhibit 1-9: A sample preview of the second page after step 11

Review questions

1 When working with a large worksheet, what command can you use to lock row or column headings in place so that when you scroll, these headings will remain visible?

2 What is the difference between freezing panes and splitting windows?

3 A worksheet can be split either horizontally or vertically, but not both simultaneously. True or False?

4 Is there a way to organize data in a worksheet so that it's grouped by levels? If so, how?

5 You can insert both vertical and horizontal page breaks in a worksheet. True or False?

Unit 2

Using multiple worksheets and workbooks

A) ctrl (hold) select sheets
to you want to print
at the same time

B) link sheets
B5 (QRT 1)
sum. North – West totals
on their sheets

B5   B5   B5   B5
NORTH SOUTH east west
need function
always start with
= (then) sum (then) (

✓ north sheet tab
shift (hold) then ✓ west tab   (fx box shows
       =Sum ('North:' West

↳ ✓ B5 and enter   then go the sheet and
copy 55 cell and paste in, remaining cells
to be calculated the same way

B) select cell r ✓, add watch , this creates
a Watch window

D) ↳ link workbooks
✓ C5, type =, go to North tab in Yearly Sales.xls
come on, enter , then go back to Overall
Sales.xls and the cell total with show up.

Unit time: 75 minutes

Complete this unit, and you'll know how to:

A Navigate, manage, and print multiple worksheets.

B Create 3-D formulas to link worksheets, and add a Watch window.

C Use the Consolidate command to summarize data from different worksheets.

D Switch between workbooks, and create and manage linked workbooks.

E Create a workspace to manage workbooks.

Topic A: Using multiple worksheets

This topic covers the following Microsoft Office Specialist exam objectives.

#	Objective
XL03S-3-4	Formatting tab color, sheet name, and background (This objective is also covered in the unit titled "Advanced formatting.")
XL03S-5-4	Organize worksheets • Inserting worksheets into a workbook • Deleting worksheets from a workbook • Repositioning worksheets in a workbook

Navigating between worksheets

Explanation

An Excel workbook can contain multiple worksheets that store related information conveniently in a single file. You can navigate between worksheets in the same workbook by using a series of sheet tabs provided at the bottom of the window, as shown in Exhibit 2-1. You can switch from one worksheet to another by clicking these tabs. You can also press Ctrl+Page Down to move to the next sheet, and press Ctrl+Page Up to move to the previous sheet in a workbook.

If your workbook contains several worksheets, Excel might not be able to display all the sheet tabs at the same time. In this case, you can use the tab scrolling buttons to reveal the hidden tabs.

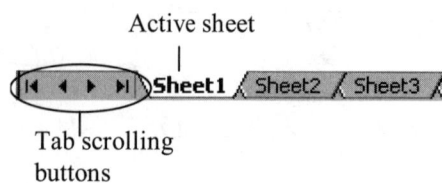

Exhibit 2-1: The sheet tabs

Do it!

A-1: Navigating between multiple worksheets

Here's how	Here's why
1 Open Navigate	(From the current unit folder.) The Navigate workbook consists of eight worksheets. Sheet1 is activated and contains the sales report for the North region for the year 2003. You can use the sheet tabs at the bottom of the workbook to switch between worksheets.
Save the workbook as **My navigate**	In the current unit folder.
2 Click the **Sheet2** tab	To view the data in the Sheet2 worksheet. It contains the 2003 sales report for the South region.
3 Activate Sheet3	(Click the Sheet3 tab.) To view the 2004 sales report for the South region.
4 Activate the Report sheet	This worksheet contains the total sales report for North and South regions for the years 2003–2005.
5 Click as shown	
	(The tab scrolling buttons are to the left of the sheet tabs.) To fully display the Consolidate sheet tab.
6 Click ◀	To display the Sheet1 tab.
7 Update the workbook	

Renaming worksheets

Explanation

By default, Excel names new worksheets consecutively as Sheet1, Sheet2, Sheet3, and so forth. You can rename these worksheets so that the names are meaningful. There are three ways to rename a worksheet:

- Double-click the sheet tab.
- Right-click the sheet tab and choose Rename.
- Choose Format, Sheet, Rename.

With any of these methods, the sheet name will be selected. Type the new name, and press Enter.

Formatting worksheet tabs

You can also color-code worksheet tabs so that it's easier to identify related sheets at a glance. Here's how:

1 Right-click the worksheet tab to display a shortcut menu.
2 Choose Tab Color to open the Format Tab Color dialog box.
3 Select the color you want to apply, and click OK.

Do it!

A-2: Naming worksheets and coloring tabs

Here's how	Here's why
1 Double-click **Sheet1**	To select the text Sheet1.
Type **North 2003**	
Press ⏎ ENTER	To change the name of the sheet to North 2003. This name identifies the contents of this sheet more specifically than Sheet1 does.
2 Right-click **Sheet2**	A shortcut menu appears.
Choose **Rename**	
Type **South 2003**	
Press ⏎ ENTER	
3 Rename Sheet3 and Sheet5 as **South 2004** and **South 2005**, respectively	(Double-click the sheet tab, enter the name, and press Enter.)
4 Rename Sheet4 and Sheet6 as **North 2004** and **North 2005**, respectively	

5 Right-click **North 2003**	(You might need to click the tab scrolling button to display the sheet.)
Choose **Tab Color...**	To open the Format Tab Color dialog box. You can color-code tabs to clearly identify related sheets.
Select the indicated color	

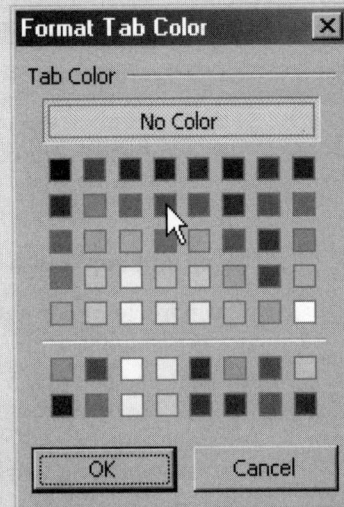

Format Tab Color

Tab Color

No Color

OK   Cancel

Click **OK**	A green line appears underlining the sheet name.
Activate the North 2004 sheet	The color of the North 2003 tab changes to green.
6 Apply the green color to the North 2004 and North 2005 tabs	(Right-click the sheet tab, and choose Tab Color.) To color both worksheet tabs green.
7 Change the color of the three South tabs to blue	(Select any shade of blue from the Format Tab Color dialog box.) The color coding helps to distinguish between the South and North region sheets.
8 Update and close the workbook	

Managing multiple worksheets

Explanation
You can insert, move, copy, and delete worksheets in a workbook. You simply follow the same procedures as you would to insert, move, copy, or delete any other data.

Inserting worksheets

When you insert a worksheet, Excel places it before the active worksheet. You can insert a new worksheet by using any of the following techniques:

- Choose Insert, Worksheet.
- Right-click the tab of the worksheet before which you want to insert the new worksheet, choose Insert, and select Worksheet from the Insert dialog box.
- Press Shift+F11.

Moving and copying worksheets

You can move or copy worksheets within a workbook, or to another workbook, by using the Move or Copy dialog box. You can also move a worksheet by dragging it to a new location. To copy a worksheet, press Ctrl and then drag the sheet to a new location.

To reposition a worksheet by using the Move or Copy dialog box:

1 Activate the worksheet you want to move.
2 Choose Edit, Move or Copy Sheet to open the Move or Copy dialog box.
3 Select a new location for the worksheet from either the To book list or the Before sheet list.
4 Click OK.

You can copy a worksheet in the same manner, except that you must check Create a copy in the Move or Copy dialog box.

Deleting worksheets

You can delete a worksheet by using the Delete command. Excel prompts you to confirm the deletion because you cannot undo this action.

To delete multiple worksheets at the same time, you need to select them. For this, click the first sheet tab, press Ctrl, and click the other sheet tabs. After selecting the worksheets, use one of the following methods:

- Choose Edit, Delete Sheet.
- Right-click the sheet tab, and choose Delete.

Do it!

A-3:   Working with multiple worksheets

Here's how	Here's why
1 Open Yearly sales	The Yearly sales workbook consists of seven worksheets. The North, South, East, and West worksheets contain the quarterly sales reports of the corresponding regions. The other three worksheets will be used for summarizing data from the individual regions.
Save the workbook as **My yearly sales**	In the current unit folder.
2 Activate the Report sheet	This worksheet contains the annual and quarterly product sales for 2004–2005.
3 Choose **Insert**, **Worksheet**	To insert a new worksheet, named Sheet1, before the Report worksheet.
4 Right-click the **Report** tab	
Choose **Insert...**	To open the Insert dialog box. The General tab is activated, and Worksheet is selected by default.
Click **OK**	To insert a new worksheet, named Sheet2, before the Report sheet.
5 Rename Sheet1 as **International**	
6 Choose **Edit**, **Move or Copy Sheet...**	To open the Move or Copy dialog box.
From the Before sheet list, select **Creating 3-D formula**	
Click **OK**	To move the International worksheet before the Creating 3-D formula worksheet.
7 Right-click the **Sheet2** tab	This sheet is not needed.
Choose **Delete**	To remove Sheet2 from the workbook.
8 Activate the International sheet	This sheet is also not needed.
Choose **Edit**, **Delete Sheet**	To remove the International sheet from the workbook.
9 Update the workbook	

Printing multiple worksheets

Explanation

You can print more than one worksheet at a time. To do so, select the worksheets that you want to print, and then click the Print button or choose File, Print. To select multiple worksheets, press and hold Ctrl, and click the tabs of the worksheets you want to select. You can also preview multiple worksheets in the same manner. You can use the Next button in the Print Preview window to move to the next worksheet in the selection.

Do it!

A-4:   Previewing and printing multiple worksheets

Here's how	Here's why
1 Activate the North sheet	(You might need to click the tab scrolling button to display this sheet.)
Press (CTRL) and click the **South**, **East**, and **West** tabs	To add the South, East, and West sheets to the selection.
Release (CTRL)	
2 Click [button]	(The Print Preview button is on the Standard toolbar.) To preview the selection.
Click **Zoom**	(If necessary.) To make the data clearly visible.
Click **Next**	To preview the South sheet.
Preview the West sheet	(Use the Next button.)
Click **Previous**	To go back to the East sheet.
3 Return to the North sheet	(Use the Previous button.)
Click **Close**	To close the preview.
4 Click [button]	(The Print button is on the Standard toolbar.) To print the selected sheets by using all the current settings.
5 Update the workbook	

Topic B: Linking worksheets by using 3-D formulas

This topic covers the following Microsoft Office Specialist exam objective.

#	Objective
XL03E-1-13	Using cell Watch

3-D formulas

Explanation

A *3-D formula* refers to the same cell or range in multiple worksheets. For example, the formula =SUM(North:West!B5) sums the data in the B5 cells for the worksheet range North:West. The syntax for referring to cells in another worksheet is:

```
worksheet_name!reference
```

Here, worksheet_name refers to the name of the worksheet that provides the data, reference is the name of the cell or range, and ! is the divider between the worksheet reference and the cell reference.

To insert a 3-D reference into a formula:

1. Enter the formula until the point where you need a value from another worksheet to complete the formula.
2. Activate the tab for the first worksheet you want to refer to.
3. While holding the Shift key, activate the tab for the last worksheet you want to refer to in the formula.
4. Select the cell or range of cells containing the values you want to refer to in the formula.
5. Complete the formula, and press Enter.

Product	Qtr1	Qtr2	Qtr3	Qtr4
Anise Seeds	$ 2,635	$ 2,036	$ 2,434	$ 2,683
Asafoetida Powder	$ 2,749	$ 2,580	$ 2,550	$ 3,233
Basil Leaf (Whole)	$ 31,677	$ 29,051	$ 23,285	$ 33,213
Bay Leaf (Whole)	$ 1,710	$ 2,718	$ 2,644	$ 2,613
Caraway Seed (Whole)	$ 2,238	$ 3,088	$ 2,372	$ 2,131
Cardamom Seed (Whole)	$ 1,246	$ 2,158	$ 1,634	$ 2,625
Cardamom Seed (Ground)	$ 2,510	$ 2,715	$ 2,574	$ 2,826
Catnip Leaf	$ 3,416	$ 1,456	$ 1,896	$ 2,962
Celery Seed (Whole)	$ 23,143	$ 28,406	$ 23,739	$ 18,349
Chamomile Flowers	$ 1,637	$ 2,584	$ 2,361	$ 2,326

Exhibit 2-2: A worksheet with 3-D formulas applied

Do it!

B-1: Creating 3-D formulas

Here's how	Here's why
1 Activate the Creating 3-D formula sheet	You'll create a formula that will sum the first-quarter sales of anise seeds for all four regions..
2 In B5, type **=SUM(**	To begin the function.
Click the **North** tab	To select the first sheet in the 3-D reference.
Press (SHIFT) and click the **West** tab	To specify the worksheet range North:West in the function. The color of the four sheet tabs in the range changes to white.
Release (SHIFT)	
Select B5 in the active worksheet	To select the cell containing the first-quarter anise seed sales in each of the four selected worksheets.
Type **)** and press (↵ ENTER)	To complete the 3-D formula.
3 Select B5	(In the Creating 3-D formula sheet.)
Observe the formula bar	= SUM(North:West!B5)
	In the formula, North:West refers to the worksheet range North through West (North, South, East, and West), ! is the divider between the worksheet and cell references, and B5 is the cell address.
4 Copy the formula in B5 to the rest of the range B6:E14	(The AutoFill Options smart tag appears.) To calculate the total quarterly sales for each product.
Deselect the text	The text will look as shown in Exhibit 2-2.
5 Update the workbook	

Adding a Watch window

Explanation

Excel formulas can refer to cells or ranges in other worksheets, or a range of worksheets, within a workbook. This type of formula creates a link between worksheets. When two worksheets are linked, any change that you make in the source cell is automatically updated in the linked cell. You can observe this effect by adding a *Watch window* to the source cell. This way, you don't need to navigate to the other worksheets to see the updated information.

To add a Watch window, right-click the cell to which you want to add it. From the shortcut menu, choose Add Watch. This opens the Watch Window toolbar, where you can view the details of the linked cell.

Do it!

B-2: Adding a Watch window

Here's how	Here's why
1 Activate the Report sheet	This worksheet contains summarized data from the North, South, East, and West worksheets.
Select B5	`= SUM(North:West!B5)`
	B5 has the value $2,635, which is the sum of all the cells with the address B5 in the worksheet range North:West. In other words, it is the total first-quarter sales of Anise Seeds from all four regions.
Right-click B5	A shortcut menu appears.
Choose **Add Watch**	To open the Watch Window toolbar. The workbook name, worksheet name, cell name, cell value, and formula in the cell appear in the Watch Window toolbar.
2 Activate the North sheet	You'll change the value of B5 in this worksheet and observe the change in the linked cell in the Watch Window toolbar.
In B5, enter **10000**	In the Watch Window toolbar, the value in B5 of the Report worksheet is updated to $12,101.
3 Close the Watch Window toolbar	
4 Update the workbook	

Topic C: Consolidating data

This topic covers the following Microsoft Office Specialist exam objective.

#	Objective
XL03E-4-5	Consolidating data from two or more worksheets

When to consolidate

Explanation

You can summarize data from different worksheets by using the data consolidation feature. Data can be consolidated either by position or by category. Consolidate by position when the related data in the source worksheets is in the same location and order. Consolidate by category when data is not in the same location and order.

The Consolidate command

To consolidate data, choose Data, Consolidate to open the Consolidate dialog box, as shown in Exhibit 2-3. The following table explains the options in this dialog box:

Option	Description
Function	Used to choose the aggregate function to consolidate data.
Reference	Used to specify the cell reference of the source data.
Browse	Used to consolidate data from different workbooks.
Use labels in	Used to include row or column headings when you consolidate data by category. When you do not check this option, Excel does not copy category labels from the source area to the destination area.
Create links to source data	Used to reflect changes made to the source data in the consolidated data.

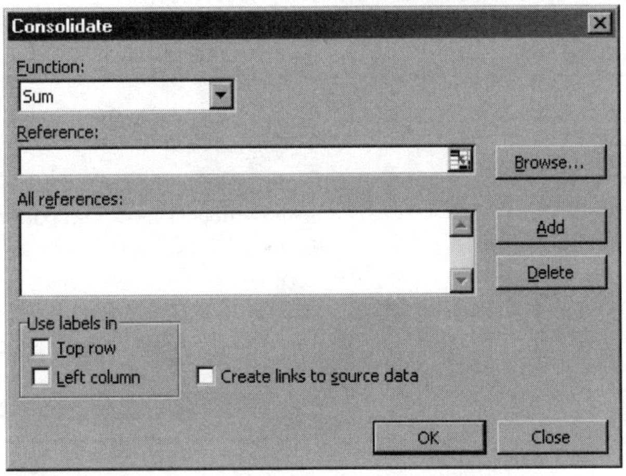

Exhibit 2-3: The Consolidate dialog box

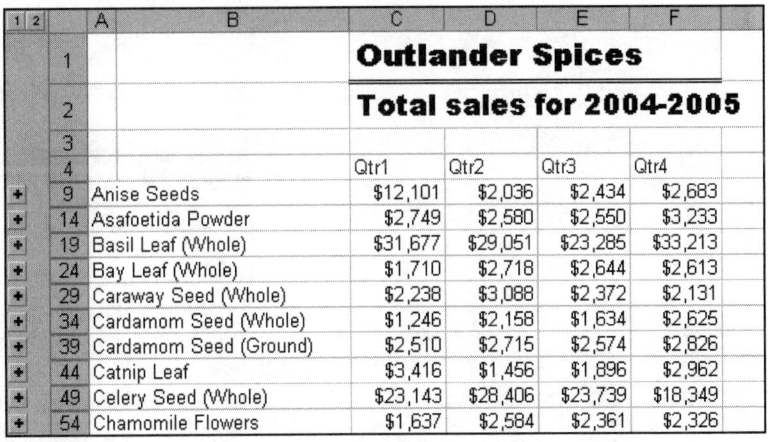

		A	B	C	D	E	F	
	1			Outlander Spices				
	2			Total sales for 2004-2005				
	3							
	4			Qtr1	Qtr2	Qtr3	Qtr4	
+	9		Anise Seeds	$12,101	$2,036	$2,434	$2,683	
+	14		Asafoetida Powder	$2,749	$2,580	$2,550	$3,233	
+	19		Basil Leaf (Whole)	$31,677	$29,051	$23,285	$33,213	
+	24		Bay Leaf (Whole)	$1,710	$2,718	$2,644	$2,613	
+	29		Caraway Seed (Whole)	$2,238	$3,088	$2,372	$2,131	
+	34		Cardamom Seed (Whole)	$1,246	$2,158	$1,634	$2,625	
+	39		Cardamom Seed (Ground)	$2,510	$2,715	$2,574	$2,826	
+	44		Catnip Leaf	$3,416	$1,456	$1,896	$2,962	
+	49		Celery Seed (Whole)	$23,143	$28,406	$23,739	$18,349	
+	54		Chamomile Flowers	$1,637	$2,584	$2,361	$2,326	

Exhibit 2-4: A worksheet with consolidated data

Do it!

C-1:   Using the Consolidate command

Here's how	Here's why
1 Activate the Consolidating data sheet	You'll use this worksheet to consolidate the sales data for all products in the four regions.
Select A4	(If necessary.) The consolidated data will begin in this cell.
Choose **Data**, **Consolidate...**	To open the Consolidate dialog box. In the Function list, Sum is selected by default.
Click ▣	Consolidate - Reference: ☒
	(The Collapse Dialog button is in the Reference box.) To collapse the Consolidate dialog box. The title of the Consolidate dialog box changes to Consolidate – Reference:, indicating that the Reference box is activated.
2 Activate the North tab	(You might have to click the navigation tab.)
Select A4:E14	**Consolidate - Reference:** North!$A$4:$E$14
	To specify the cell range. This range includes the product and quarter labels. The Consolidate – Reference: box reads North!$A$4:$E$14.
Click ▣	(The Collapse Dialog button is in the Consolidate-Reference dialog box.) To expand the Consolidate dialog box.
Click **Add**	To add North!$A$4:$E$14 to the All references list.
3 Click the **South** tab	To create a reference to the South worksheet. Notice that the cell range A4:E14 is selected. Excel takes the cell or range specified in the last reference as the default for the new reference. The value South!$A$4:$E$14 appears in the Reference box.
Click **Add**	To add South!$A$4:$E$14 to the All references list.
4 Add the references from the East and West worksheets to the All references list	

5	Under Use labels in, check **Top row**	(The Consolidating data worksheet becomes activated.) You'll consolidate data based on the labels in the top row. Excel copies the labels to the destination area when you consolidate data.
	Under Use labels in, check **Left column**	You'll consolidate data based on the labels in the left column.
	Check **Create links to source data**	To update the data automatically when changes are made to the source data.
	Click **OK**	To close the Consolidate dialog box.
6	Deselect the cells	The worksheet shows the total product sales by quarter for the four regions. Outline symbols appear to the left of the worksheet. The worksheet will resemble Exhibit 2-4.

7 Click the row-level expand symbol next to row 9

		Qtr1	Qtr2	Qtr3	Qtr4
5	My Yearly Sales	$734	$457	$327	$235
6	My Yearly Sales	$10,000	$423	$521	$625
7	My Yearly Sales	$833	$733	$1,065	$1,198
8	My Yearly Sales	$534	$423	$521	$625

To display the total sales of anise seeds by region. The total sales figure for each region is listed in the order you specified in the Consolidate dialog box. Excel uses the name of the workbook, "My Yearly Sales," as the labels for the detail rows.

Select C9

`=SUM(C5:C8)`

The formula bar shows that the value in C9 is the result of adding C5:C8.

Select C5

`=East!$B$5`

The formula bar shows the formula containing a link to the East worksheet.

8 Update and close the workbook

Topic D: Linking workbooks

Explanation

Just as you can link multiple worksheets within a workbook, you can also link multiple workbooks. You can do this by writing a formula in one workbook that refers to a cell, range, or name in another workbook. References to other workbooks are called *external references*. You can maintain workbook links—even if the workbook that is referred to is renamed—by using the Edit, Link command.

Using multiple workbooks

You can open and work with as many workbooks as your computer memory permits. Each workbook has its own window and a unique button on the taskbar. To switch between workbooks, choose the workbook name from the Window menu, or simply click the workbook's taskbar button.

Do it!

D-1: Switching between workbooks

Here's how	Here's why
1 Open Yearly sales	(Note that you are opening Yearly sales and not My yearly sales.)
Open Overall sales	
	A separate button for each workbook appears on the taskbar. (Your taskbar might look different depending on the files that are open and the items in the Quick Launch.)
2 Click the **Yearly sales** taskbar button	To activate the Yearly sales workbook.
3 Choose **Window**	
	The names of the two open workbooks appear, and the active workbook is selected.
Choose **Overall sales**	To activate the Overall sales workbook.
4 Save the workbook as **My overall sales**	In the current unit folder.

External links

Explanation

The syntax for referring to cells in another workbook is:

```
'[workbook_name]worksheet_name'!reference
```

Here, workbook_name refers to the name of the workbook that provides the data, and worksheet_name refers to the name of the worksheet in the source workbook. At the end of the formula, reference is the name of the cell or range, and ! is the divider between the worksheet reference and the cell reference.

Do it!

D-2: Examining external links in a worksheet

Here's how	Here's why
1 Activate the Quarterly revenue sheet	(If necessary.) This worksheet contains the quarterly revenue report for 2004–2005. The My overall sales workbook is linked to the Yearly sales workbook. Column C of the Quarterly revenue worksheet contains total sales for the first quarter.
Select C6	='[Yearly sales.xls]North'!$B$15
	In the formula, Yearly sales refers to the source workbook, North is the name of the worksheet, and $B$15 is the cell address to which the formula is linked. The current value in this cell is 14074.
2 Activate the Yearly sales workbook	(Use the Window menu.) The North worksheet is activated.
In B5, enter **1000**	The value in B15 changes from $14,074 to $14,540.
3 Activate the My overall sales workbook	To view the changes in the linked workbook. In the Quarterly revenue worksheet, the value in C6 has changed from 14074 to 14540.
4 Update the My overall sales workbook	

Creating external links

Explanation

You can build formulas that refer to worksheets in other workbooks. This type of reference is called an external reference or *external link*. The workbook that contains the formula is called the *destination workbook*, and the workbook to which the formula refers to is called the *source workbook*.

To create an external link:

1 Open the destination workbook.

2 Click the cell in which the formula is to be entered.

3 Type the formula with a reference to the source workbook, and press Enter.

Region	Total expenses	Total sales	Profit/Loss
North	$13,395	$62,216	$48,821
South	$89,000	$88,358	($642)
East	$21,947	$76,345	$54,398
West	$15,530	$61,750	$46,220

Exhibit 2-5: A worksheet with external references

Do it!

D-3: Creating external links in a worksheet

Here's how	Here's why
1 Activate the Total revenue sheet	You'll create a new link between the My overall sales workbook and the Yearly sales workbook. The Profit/Loss column displays profit or loss for each region. Currently, the Total sales column does not contain any data.
2 In C5, enter **=**	
Activate the Yearly sales workbook	The North worksheet is activated.
Select F15	='[Yearly sales.xls]North'!$F$15
	To enter a linked reference. Yearly sales refers to the workbook name, North refers to the worksheet name, and $F$15 is the cell reference.
Press ⏎ ENTER	To enter the external reference. The My overall sales worksheet becomes active. C5 shows the result of the formula, which is $62,216.
3 Enter the external references for the remaining regions	(Remember to enter these as linked references.) Activate the respective region tabs of the Yearly sales workbook, select the total sales value in F15, and press Enter. The worksheet will resemble Exhibit 2-5.
4 Update the My overall sales workbook	

Maintaining workbook links

Explanation

You might want to change the name of a workbook that is linked to another workbook. If both the source and destination workbooks are open, the link gets updated automatically. If you don't have the destination workbook open, you can still redirect the links by using the Edit, Links command.

To redirect links:

1 Choose Edit, Links to open the Edit Links dialog box.

2 From the Source file list, select the source workbook whose links you want to redirect.

3 Click the Change Source button to open the Change Source dialog box.

4 Select the name of the workbook to which you want to redirect the link. Click OK to return to the Edit Links dialog box.

5 Click OK to close the Edit Links dialog box.

Do it!

D-4: Editing links

Here's how	Here's why
1 Select C5	`='[Yearly sales.xls]North'!$F$15`
	(In the Total revenue sheet of the My overall sales workbook.) The formula in the formula bar contains a reference to the Yearly sales workbook.
2 Activate the Yearly sales workbook	
Save the Yearly sales workbook as **Regional sales**	(Use the File, Save As command to save the file with a different name.) Saving the source file with a different name will automatically update the link in the destination file.
3 Activate the My overall sales workbook	
Select C5	`='[Regional sales.xls]North'!$F$15`
	(If necessary.) To view the updated link. The formula now contains a reference to the Regional sales workbook instead of to the Yearly sales workbook.
4 Update and close the My overall sales workbook	
5 Save the Regional sales workbook as **New regional sales**	

6 Open My overall sales	**Microsoft Excel** [X] ⚠ This workbook contains links to other data sources. • If you update the links, Excel attempts to retrieve the latest data. • If you don't update, Excel uses the previous information. [Update] [Don't Update] [Help]
	Excel displays a message box prompting you to update the linked information.
Click **Update**	To update the destination workbook with the latest information.
7 Select C5	(If necessary.) The formula still refers to Regional sales.xls.
Choose **Edit**, **Links...**	To open the Edit Links dialog box. The name of the source workbook is shown as Regional sales.xls.
Click **Change Source**	To open the Change Source: Regional sales.xls dialog box.
From the list of files, double-click **New regional sales**	In the source file list, the name of the source workbook has changed to New regional sales.xls.
Click **Close**	='[New regional sales.xls]North'!$F$15
	The reference to Regional sales.xls has changed to New regional sales.xls.
8 Update the My overall sales workbook	

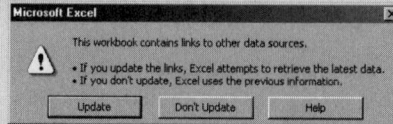

Topic E: Managing workbooks

This topic covers the following Microsoft Office Specialist exam objective.

#	Objective
XL03S-5-6	Customize window layout
	• Splitting and arranging workbooks
	• Splitting, freezing/unfreezing, arranging and hiding/unhiding workbooks (This objective is also covered in the unit titled "Working with large worksheets.")

Workspaces

Explanation

If you find that you repeatedly work with the same set of workbooks, you can save them as a workspace. A *workspace* is a logical container of related workbooks that retains page setups, window sizes, and display settings. A workspace does not save the workbooks themselves, so you'll still need to save changes in each workbook individually.

Creating workspaces

While working with multiple workbooks, you can arrange them in a specific way on the screen to maximize the data you can see. Excel calls this arrangement a *workspace.* You can save this arrangement in a workspace file, which stores the position and size of the window for each open workbook. By default, Excel saves the workspace file as resume.xlw. You can rename the file if you use different workspace files for different workbooks.

To create a workspace:

1   Open all the workbooks that you want to save as a workspace.
2   Set the window sizes, screen magnifications, and any other display settings as you want them to be whenever you open the workspace.
3   Choose File, Save Workspace to open the Save Workspace dialog box.
4   Specify a name and location for the workspace, and then click the Save button.

To open a workspace, select it from the Open dialog box.

Hiding and unhiding workbooks

If you have multiple workbooks open either individually or as part of a workspace, you can hide or unhide the workbooks of your choice. To hide a workbook, select the workbook and choose Window, Hide. To unhide a workbook, choose Window, Unhide and from the Unhide dialog box, select the window you want to display and click OK.

E-1: Creating a workspace

Here's how	Here's why
1 Choose **Window, Arrange...**	To open the Arrange Windows dialog box.
Select **Vertical**	
Click **OK**	Notice that all the open workbooks are vertically arranged on screen.
2 Activate the My overall sales workbook	(If necessary.)
Change the magnification to **75%**	
3 Change the magnification for the New regional sales workbook to **75%**	
4 Choose **File, Save Workspace...**	To open the Save Workspace dialog box. By default, Workspaces is selected in the Save as type list.
Navigate to the current unit folder	(If necessary.)
Observe the default name in the File name box	Resume appears as the default name.
Edit the File name box to read **My sales**	
Click **Save**	To save the workspace.
5 Close all open workbooks	(If a message box appears asking to save workbook changes, click Yes.)
6 Display the Open dialog box	
Select **My sales**	
Click **Open**	The New regional sales and My yearly sales workbooks appear just as they did when you saved the workspace.
7 Open My navigate	You'll add another workbook to the workspace.
8 Activate My overall sales	

9	Choose **Window**, **Arrange...**	To open the Arrange Windows dialog box.
	Select **Tiled**	
	Click **OK**	To close the dialog box and tile the open windows.
10	Open the Save Workspace dialog box	(Choose File, Save Workspace.) In the File name box, My sales is selected.
	Click **Save**	A message box asks if you want to replace the existing workspace.
	Click **Yes**	(If a message box appears asking to save workbook changes, click Yes.)
11	Close all open workbooks	
12	Open My sales	The three workbooks appear as they did when you saved the workspace.
13	Close all open workbooks	If you're prompted to save changes, click No.

Unit summary: Using multiple worksheets and workbooks

Topic A   In this topic, you learned how to **navigate between multiple worksheets** and how to improve worksheet identification by **renaming worksheets** and adding **color** to their **tabs**. You also learned how to **insert**, **copy**, **move**, and **delete worksheets** and how to **preview** and **print** multiple worksheets.

Topic B   In this topic, you learned how to create **3-D formulas** to perform calculations across multiple worksheets. You also learned that Excel automatically updates the data in **destination** cells if you change the data in the **source** cells. You observed this in the **Watch Window toolbar** without navigating between worksheets.

Topic C   In this topic, you learned how to use the **Consolidate command** to summarize data from several ranges. You learned that you can consolidate by position or by category and that you can create links to the source data.

Topic D   In this topic, you learned how to create **external links** to data in another workbook. You learned how data is automatically updated in the destination workbook when you change the data in the source workbook. You also learned how to use the **Edit Links dialog box** to change links in destination workbooks.

Topic E   In this topic, you saved the display settings of several workbooks as a **workspace**, making it easier to open and work on them simultaneously.

Independent practice activity

1 Open Practice sales 2004-2005 (from the current unit folder), and save it as **My practice sales 2004-2005**. Open Product (from the current unit folder), and save it as **My Product**.

2 Activate the Report worksheet of the My practice sales 2004-2005 workbook.

3 Create 3-D formulas to calculate the total sales (in $) for all products in all four regions. The formula for calculating total sales is **Qty Sold * Price**. Qty Sold for each region is stored in the respective region worksheets of the My Practice sales 2004-2005 workbook. Prices are stored in the My Product workbook. (*Hint:* To do this for the North region, in My Practice sales 2004-2005, activate Report, and type = in B5. In My Product, select C5. Remove the $ sign before C & 5 in the formula bar. Then, type * after C5 in the formula bar. Click the **North** tab in My Practice Sales 2004-2005, select B5, and press Enter. Use AutoFill to obtain the values for the rest of the Products under North.)

   Using the same technique, create formulas for C5:E5, and use AutoFill to obtain the values for each of the remaining regions. When you're done, compare your results with Exhibit 2-6.

4 Update the My practice sales 2004-2005 workbook, and close it. Close the My Product workbook.

5 Open the Yearly sales and Overall sales workbooks. Activate the Quarterly revenue worksheet of the Overall sales workbook. Verify that the Quarterly revenue worksheet is linked to the Yearly sales workbook.

6 Change the name of the Yearly sales workbook to **Annual sales**.

7 Verify that the source of the link is updated in the Overall sales workbook.

8 Arrange the open workbooks horizontally in the Excel window.

9 Create a workspace named **My practice sales** that saves the current display settings.

10 Update and close both workbooks.

	A	B	C	D	E
1		**Outlander Spices**			
2		**Total sales (in $) for 2004-2005**			
3					
4	Product	North	South	East	West
5	Cassia	$ 5,372,210.26	$ 2,773,021.82	$ 2,646,600.39	$ 5,025,111.81
6	Catnip Leaf	$ 5,861,989.90	$ 1,218,444.35	$ 3,025,700.98	$ 2,747,249.91
7	Celery Seed (Whole)	$ 383,650.11	$ 677,864.95	$ 328,505.11	$ 909,246.19
8	Celery Seed (Ground)	$ 4,198,896.69	$ 2,614,144.22	$ 4,363,486.90	$ 3,265,664.78
9	Chamomile Flowers	$ 69,156.44	$ 286,677.15	$ 492,054.57	$ 253,668.88
10	Chili Pepper Powder	$ 2,266,211.90	$ 5,544,111.26	$ 4,082,834.29	$ 2,125,810.94
11	Chinese Star Anise (Ground)	$ 1,922,761.01	$ 4,358,487.41	$ 2,488,171.25	$ 473,144.84
12	Chinese Star Anise (Whole)	$ 697,750.28	$ 7,128,062.44	$ 931,405.70	$ 4,509,600.89
13	Chives	$ 7,725,468.11	$ 4,092,268.77	$ 2,398,023.46	$ 448,907.65
14	Cilantro Flakes	$ 7,938,852.74	$ 2,884,556.52	$ 1,442,793.30	$ 1,953,937.24

Exhibit 2-6: A sample of the My practice sales 2004-2005 workbook after Step 3 of the Independent Practice Activity

Review questions

1 List three methods you can use to change a worksheet name.

2 What is the advantage of a Watch window?

3 How do you add a Watch window to observe a cell?

4 What is a workspace?

5 When you save a workspace are the workbooks themselves also saved individually?

Unit 3

Customizing Excel

adding & removing commands

Tools ↳ Customize

Topic A: Using the Options dialog box

This topic covers the following Microsoft Office Specialist exam objectives.

#	Objective
XL03E-5-3	Modifying default font settings
XL03E-5-3	Setting the default number of worksheets

Overview

Explanation

You can use the Options dialog box to change some aspects of how you interact with Excel. For example, you might want to change the format in which data appears on screen, or turn off the gridlines around cells. You can use this dialog box to change the default settings of various option categories, such as View, General, and Calculation.

View options

You can use the View tab in the Options dialog box to change the way Excel displays data. You can also control other aspects of the Excel environment, including toolbars, the menu bar, and the status bar.

To change the view settings, choose Tools, Options to open the Options dialog box. Activate the View tab. Select any of the settings and click OK. Exhibit 3-1 shows the Options dialog box with the View tab activated.

The following table explains the groups of options you can set by using the View tab:

Group	Description
Show	Contains options to show or hide the formula bar, status bar, and Startup task pane when Excel is launched, and to specify whether each Excel window will have its own taskbar button.
Comments	Contains three options that are used to hide and display comments and comment indicators.
Objects	Contains three options that are used to display or hide graphic objects in a worksheet.
Window options	Contains various view options, such as Gridlines, Zero values, and Sheet tabs, which are applied only to the active window.

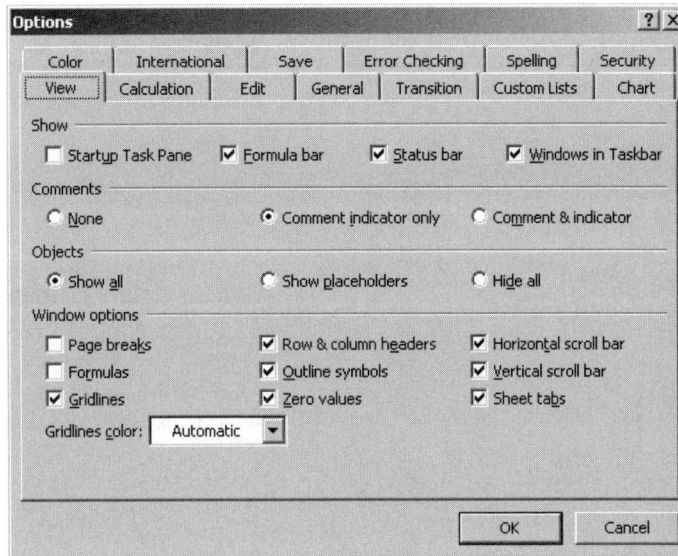

Exhibit 3-1: The View tab in the Options dialog box

Do it!

A-1: Changing view options

Here's how	Here's why
1 Open Customize	From the current unit folder.
Save the workbook as **My customize**	In the current unit folder.
Verify that the Sales worksheet is active	The Sales worksheet contains quarterly sales data for products during 2004–2005. You'll change the view options for this workbook.
2 Select F5	This formula adds the range B5:E5 and displays the result in the cell.
3 Choose **Tools, Options...**	To open the Options dialog box. By default, the View tab is active.
Under Window options, check **Formulas**	To display formulas, instead of the results they produce, in cells.
Click **OK**	

Total sales
=SUM(B5:E5)
=SUM(B6:E6)
=SUM(B7:E7)

	(The Formula Auditing toolbar appears.) The formulas for Total sales and Quarterly sales are displayed in the cells. Column width also increases. Use the Formulas setting when you want to track down errors in formulas.
4 Open the Options dialog box	(Choose Tools, Options.)
Under Window options, clear **Formulas**	
Click **OK**	The Total sales column and the Quarterly sales row show values instead of formulas. Columns return to their original width.
5 Open the Options dialog box	
Under Window options, clear **Gridlines**	
Click **OK**	The gridlines on this worksheet disappear.
6 Activate the Revenue sheet	The gridlines are still visible on this worksheet. Changes in view options are applied to only the current worksheet.
7 Return to the Sales sheet	
8 Update the workbook	

General options

Explanation   You can change other workbook settings by using the General tab in the Options dialog box, as shown in Exhibit 3-2. General options are applied to all new workbooks. The following table explains some of the options you'll find on this tab:

Option	Description
R1C1 reference style	Changes the cell reference style from A1 to R1C1. In A1 style, columns are labeled alphabetically, and rows are labeled numerically. In R1C1 style, both rows and columns are labeled numerically (R stands for row and C stands for column).
Web Options	Displays the Web Options dialog box, in which you can set options that determine how the worksheet will look in a Web browser.
Sheets in new workbook	Specifies the number of worksheets that will be included automatically in new workbooks.
Standard font	Specifies the default font of new workbooks. You can modify the default font and font size by using the Standard font and Size drop-down lists. However, changes in font and font size are reflected only after you restart Excel.

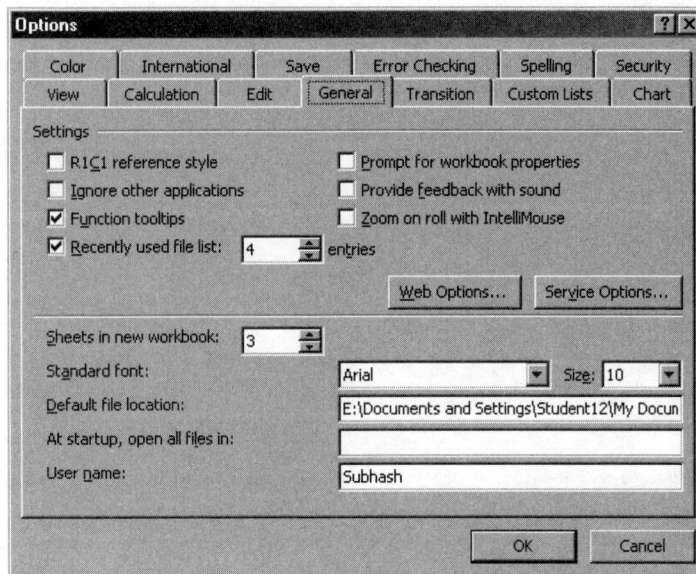

Exhibit 3-2: The General tab in the Options dialog box

Do it!

A-2:   Changing general options

Here's how	Here's why
1 Select A1	The Name box in the upper-left region of the worksheet contains the cell reference A1.
2 Open the Options dialog box	
Click the **General** tab	
Under Settings, check **R1C1 reference style**	
Click **OK**	
	The column labels change from letters to numbers. In the Name box, the cell reference style changes from A1 to R1C1. You can use this reference style when writing Visual Basic Application procedures.
3 Open Practice customize	(From the current unit folder.) The R1C1 reference style is applied to this workbook. Any change in general options is applied to all new workbooks.
Close Practice customize	
4 Change the cell reference style back to the default	(Open the Options dialog box, and clear R1C1 reference style.)
Click **OK**	To close the dialog box. The columns in the worksheet are again labeled alphabetically.
5 Choose **File**	To display the list of commands in the File menu. The File menu displays the names of the four files accessed most recently on your computer.
Close the menu	(Click anywhere in the worksheet.)
6 Open the Options dialog box	By default, the Recently used file list entries box shows 4.
Edit the Recently used file list entries box to read **1**	To specify that Excel shows only one file in the File menu.
Click **OK**	

7 Display the File menu	There is now only one file name at the bottom of the File menu.
Close the menu	
8 Open the Options dialog box	
Observe the Standard font and Size lists	Use these options to change the default font and font size of workbooks created from this point forward. After selecting a new standard font or font size, you must close and restart Excel before these changes can be applied to a new workbook.
Close the Options dialog box	

Calculation options

Calculation is the process of computing and displaying the results of formulas. You can set Excel to perform calculations automatically or only when triggered manually by the user. By default, Excel calculates the formulas automatically. When Calculation is set to Automatic, the values in some cells change when values in related cells are changed. To set calculation options, you can use the Calculation tab in the Options dialog box, as shown in Exhibit 3-3.

The following table explains some of the options available on the Calculation tab:

Option	Description
Automatic	Calculates all dependent formulas whenever you change any value, formula, or name. This is the default setting.
Automatic except tables	Calculates all dependent formulas automatically except data tables. Data tables are calculated only when you click the Calc Sheet button.
Manual	Calculates all open workbooks only when you click the Calc Now (F9) button. When you select this setting, Excel makes the Recalculate before save option available. This option will automatically recalculate the worksheet before you save it.
Calc Now (F9)	Calculates all open worksheets. It also calculates data tables and updates all open chart sheets.
Calc Sheet	Calculates only the active worksheet. It also calculates the charts and chart sheets that are linked to the active worksheet.

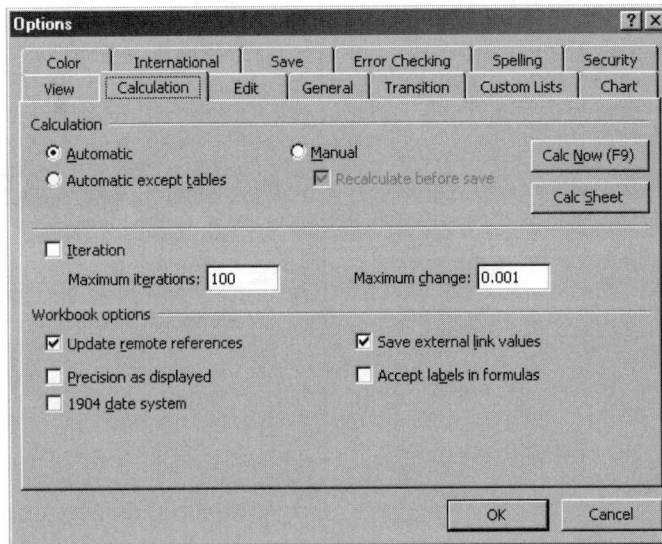

Exhibit 3-3: The Calculation tab in the Options dialog box

Do it!

A-3: Changing calculation options

Here's how	Here's why
1 Observe the Sales sheet	The Sales worksheet uses formulas to calculate the total sales and quarterly sales figures. B13 contains a formula that adds the cell range B5:B12. The value in B13 is $19,993.
Activate the Revenue sheet	This worksheet contains a linking formula in the Total Sales column. This formula links the Revenue worksheet with the Sales worksheet.
2 Open the Options dialog box	
Click the **Calculation** tab	Under Calculation, Automatic is selected by default. This means that Excel will calculate all dependent formulas when any value is changed. The Recalculate before save check box is disabled.
Close the Options dialog box	(Click OK.)
3 Activate the Sales sheet	(If necessary.)
In B5, enter **30000**	The value in B13 changes to 40,398 automatically.
Activate the Revenue sheet	B5 contains the new value.
4 Open the Options dialog box	
Click the **Calculation** tab	(If necessary.)
Under Calculation, select **Manual**	To calculate the values of the open workbooks only when you click the Calc Now button or press the F9 key. You can click the Calc Sheet button to calculate only the active sheet. The Recalculate before save check box is now available and checked by default. This setting tells Excel to calculate all formulas automatically when you save the workbook.
Click **OK**	
5 Select B5	(In the Revenue sheet.) This cell contains a link to the Sales worksheet. The value in B5 is $40,398.
6 Activate the Sales sheet	You'll change a value in this worksheet and view the impact of the change on calculated values in the Revenue worksheet.
In B5, enter **20000**	The value in B13 does not change. This tells you that Excel did not calculate the worksheet after you changed the value.

7	Activate the Revenue sheet	The value in B5 has not changed.
	Activate the Sales sheet	
8	Open the Options dialog box	
	Click **Calc Sheet**	To calculate the active worksheet manually. The value in B13 changes to $30,398.
9	Activate the Revenue sheet	B5 still shows the previous value because clicking the Calc Sheet button performs the calculations for only the active worksheet.
10	Activate the Sales sheet	
	In B6, enter **15000**	The value in B13 does not change.
11	Open the Options dialog box	
	Click **Calc Now (F9)**	To perform the calculation on all open worksheets. The value in B13 has changed to $44,766.
	Activate the Revenue sheet	The value in B5 also changes to $44,766.
12	Open the Options dialog box	
	Set the Calculation option back to Automatic	(Under Calculation, select Automatic.)
	Click **OK**	
13	Update the workbook	

Topic B: Customizing toolbars and menus

This topic covers the following Microsoft Office Specialist exam objectives.

#	Objective
XL03E-5-1	Adding and removing buttons from toolbars
XL03E-5-1	Adding custom menus

Overview

Explanation

Excel has several built-in toolbars and menus. Some of the toolbars, such as Standard and Formatting, appear automatically when you start Excel. You can customize toolbars by adding, removing, and moving buttons you use frequently. Excel automatically saves any changes you make to the toolbars and menus.

Showing and hiding a toolbar

You might want to add more toolbars to the program window than are currently shown. To show or hide a toolbar, right-click any visible toolbar or menu bar, and select the name of the toolbar you want to show or hide. You can also use the Toolbars tab in the Customize dialog box, or choose View, Toolbars, <submenu>, where <submenu> represents the name of the toolbar to be hidden or displayed.

Do it!

B-1: Showing and hiding toolbars

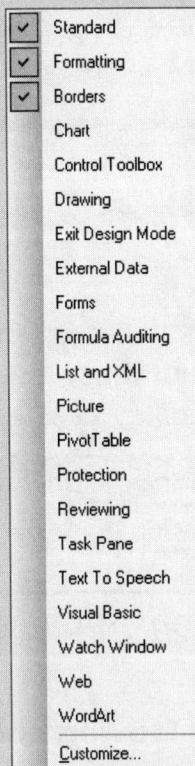

Here's how	Here's why
1 Right-click the Standard toolbar	☑ Standard ☑ Formatting ☑ Borders Chart Control Toolbox Drawing Exit Design Mode External Data Forms Formula Auditing List and XML Picture PivotTable Protection Reviewing Task Pane Text To Speech Visual Basic Watch Window Web WordArt Customize...
	To display the toolbar shortcut menu. You can right-click anywhere on the toolbar or menu bar to display this shortcut menu. The check marks in front of Standard, Formatting, and Borders indicate that these are the only toolbars currently visible.
Choose **Chart**	To display the Chart toolbar.
2 Display the shortcut menu for toolbars	(Right-click on any toolbar or menu bar.) A check mark appears in front of the Chart option.
Choose **Chart**	The Chart toolbar disappears.

Moving and docking a toolbar

Explanation

Toolbars can appear in one of two states: docked or floating. *Docked* toolbars are attached to an edge of the program window. *Floating* toolbars appear floating over the worksheet. You can move either type of toolbar by dragging it to a new location. Exhibit 3-4 displays both docked and floating toolbars.

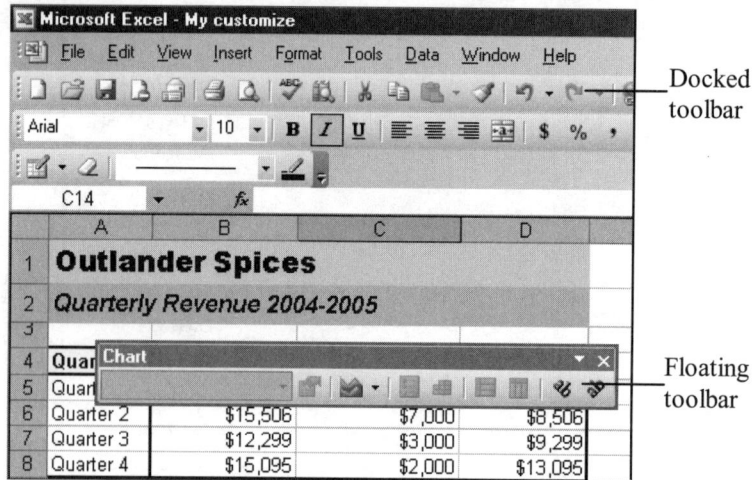

Exhibit 3-4: Docked and floating toolbars

Do it!

B-2: Moving and docking toolbars

Here's how	Here's why
1 Point to the left edge of the Standard toolbar	
	(The shape of the pointer changes to a four-headed arrow.) You'll move the Standard toolbar, which is docked below the menu bar.
Drag the Standard toolbar onto the worksheet	To make the toolbar float over the worksheet.
2 Drag the Standard toolbar to the right edge of the worksheet	(Drag it by its title bar.) To dock the Standard toolbar vertically on the right side of the worksheet. You can dock toolbars on any side of the program window.
3 Dock the Standard toolbar below the menu bar	To return the toolbar to its default position.

Customizing toolbars

Explanation   You might use certain commands that are not represented by buttons on any of Excel's default toolbars. You can customize your toolbars by adding and deleting buttons to include such commands.

To add a button:

1   Choose Tools, Customize to open the Customize dialog box.

2   Click the Commands tab.

3   From the Categories list, select the category of the command you want to add to a toolbar.

4   Drag the command you want from the Commands list onto a toolbar of your choice. As you drag, an insertion line indicates where the button will appear when you drop it.

To remove a button from a toolbar, open the Customize dialog box, and drag the button off the toolbar.

Restoring toolbars

You can also reset a toolbar to its original state. To do this:

1   Open the Customize dialog box.

2   Click the Toolbars tab, and select the toolbar that you want to restore to its default settings.

3   Click Reset.

4   Click OK to confirm that you want to reset the selected toolbar. Click Close to close the Customize dialog box.

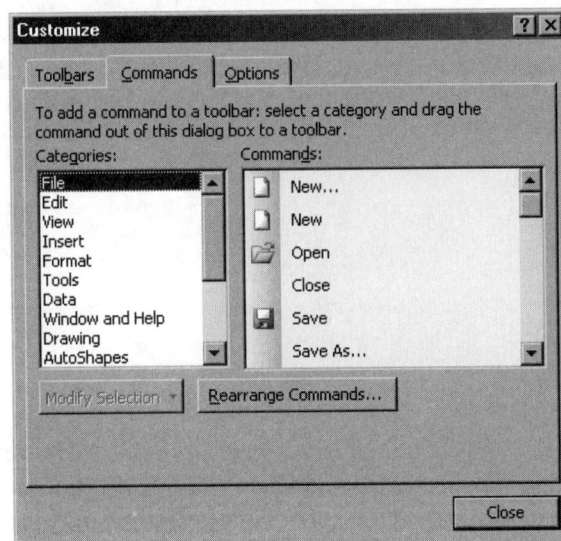

Exhibit 3-5: The Customize dialog box

Do it!

B-3: Customizing and restoring toolbars

Here's how	Here's why
1 Choose **Tools**, **Customize...**	To open the Customize dialog box.
2 Click the **Commands** tab	You can view the available menu categories and their associated commands, as shown in Exhibit 3-5.
3 From the Categories list, select **Edit**	To display the commands available in the Edit category.
From the Commands list, select **Delete**	
Drag **Delete** from the Commands list to the Standard toolbar as shown	
4 Click **Close**	
	The Delete button now appears on the Standard toolbar.
5 Display the toolbar shortcut menu	
Choose **Customize...**	To open the Customize dialog box. While this dialog box is open, you can drag buttons to new positions on the toolbars.
6 Drag the Format Painter button to a new position as shown	
	The position of the Format Painter button changes.

7 Click the **Toolbars** tab

Observe the New button

(The New Button is on the Customize dialog box.) You can use this button to create your own custom toolbars.

From the Toolbars list, check **Standard**

(If necessary.) Make sure you do *not* clear the Standard check box, because doing so will hide the toolbar.

Click **Reset**

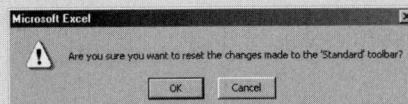

Excel prompts you to confirm that you want to reset the selected toolbar.

Click **OK**

To reset the Standard toolbar.

Observe the Standard toolbar

The Delete button no longer appears, and the Format Painter button appears in its original position.

8 Click **Close**

Customizing menus

Explanation

As with toolbars, you can also customize menus by adding or deleting commands. To customize a menu:

1 Display the Commands tab in the Customize dialog box.

2 From the Categories list, select the category containing the command you want to add to a menu.

3 From the Commands list, select the command you want to add.

4 Drag the selected command to the relevant menu. When you drag the command to a menu or submenu, the menu or submenu opens, and you can place the command in it.

Do it!

B-4: Customizing a menu

Here's how	Here's why
1 Open the Customize dialog box	(Choose Tools, Customize.)
Activate the Commands tab	
2 Display the Format menu	(In the Excel window.) You might have to drag the Customize dialog box to the right to view the Format menu and the Customize dialog box at the same time.
3 From the Categories list, select **Format**	To display the commands in the Format category.
From the Commands list, select **Erase Border**	You'll add this menu command to the Format menu.
Drag the Erase Border command from the Commands list to the indicated location	
	The Erase Border command appears in the Format menu.
4 Click **Close**	(In the Customize dialog box.) To close the dialog box.

Short menus and smart menus

Explanation

Excel menus are referred to as *short menus* if they do not display all the available commands when you first open them. To view all the commands, you have to either wait several seconds or click the down chevron at the bottom of the menu, as shown in Exhibit 3-6.

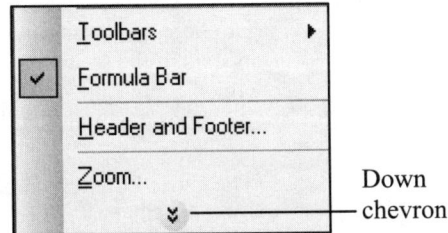

Exhibit 3-6: A sample short menu and the down chevron

If you want, you can turn off this feature by using the Options tab in the Customize dialog box. To do so:

1 Choose Tools, Customize.

2 Activate the Options tab.

3 Check Always show full menus.

4 Click Close.

When you start Excel for the first time and use different commands for a while, Excel changes the menus to display the commands that you use most frequently. This feature is called *smart menus*.

Do it!

B-5:   Exploring short menus and smart menus

Here's how	Here's why
1 Choose **View**	To display the View menu. A chevron appears at the bottom of the menu. The commands in the menu appear automatically after a short delay.
Choose **Full Screen**	(Or choose another command if this one already appears in the short menu.) To view the worksheet in Full Screen mode. A floating Full Screen toolbar appears on the worksheet.
2 Click **Close Full Screen**	(The Close Full Screen button is on the Full Screen toolbar.) To display the worksheet in Normal view.
3 Choose **View**	The Full Screen command now appears in the short menu.
4 Open the Customize dialog box	
Click the **Options** tab	
Check **Always show full menus**	To specify that Excel should display a complete list of commands every time you select a menu.
Click **Close**	
5 Choose **View**	The menu displays all the available View commands. The down chevron does not appear.
6 Update and close the workbook	

Unit summary: Customizing Excel

Topic A In this topic, you learned how to change Excel's **View**, **General**, and **Calculation** settings. You learned how to **set** or **change** these options by using the **Options dialog box**.

Topic B In this topic, you learned how to **customize toolbars** and **menus**. You also learned how to **move** and **dock** toolbars. You learned how to **add** a **toolbar button** and **menu command**. In addition, you learned how to use the **Reset** command to reset toolbars.

Independent practice activity

1 Open Practice customize.

2 Change the color of the gridlines to blue. (*Hint:* Use the Gridlines color palette in the View options tab.)

3 Change the General settings to display two recently used files in the File menu.

4 Change the Calculation option to Manual.

5 Change the values in the Initial quantity and Quantity sold columns. Observe the impact of these changes. Calculate the values in the workbook manually.

6 Change the Calculation option to Automatic.

7 Move the Formatting toolbar so that it floats over the worksheet.

8 Dock the Formatting toolbar in its original location (below the Standard toolbar).

9 Add the Save As button to the Formatting toolbar. (*Hint:* In the Commands tab of the Customize dialog box, under Categories, select File. Under Commands, select Save As.)

10 Reset the Formatting toolbar to restore it to its original state.

11 Close the workbook (you don't need to save changes).

Review questions

1 List some groups of View options that you can change using the Options dialog box?

2 On which tab in the Options dialog box can you change the default number of worksheets and default font settings for new files?

3 What is manual calculation?

4 What is meant by the term "docked toolbar?"

5 List the steps you would use to customize a menu by adding a new comand.

Unit 4

Advanced formatting

today date function
= NOW( )   *} = today's*
                date
              formula

Unit time: 75 minutes

Complete this unit, and you'll know how to:

A Add borders and shading to a worksheet to emphasize data and improve worksheet appearance and readability.

B Apply built-in and custom number formats to display data in specific formats, and format cells based on conditions.

C Work with date and time formats, and perform calculations on dates.

D Create, apply, and modify styles to apply several kinds of formatting simultaneously.

E Merge and change orientation of cells to display text in special ways.

Topic A: Borders and shading

This topic covers the following Microsoft Office Specialist exam objective.

#	Objective
XL03S-3-4	Formatting tab color, sheet name, and background (This objective is also covered in the unit titled "Using multiple worksheets and workbooks.")

Borders

Explanation

To distinguish between different types of data in a worksheet, you can apply borders, shading, or both to cells. You apply a border by selecting a cell or range and then selecting a border from the Borders palette. To display the Borders palette, click the arrow next to the Borders button on the Formatting toolbar.

You can also apply borders by using the Border tab in the Format Cells dialog box. To remove borders from a selected range, select No Border from the Borders palette.

Do it!

A-1:   Adding borders to a cell or range

Here's how	Here's why
1 Open Advanced formatting	From the current unit folder.
Save the workbook as **My advanced formatting**	In the current unit folder.
Observe the Sales sheet	The data appears organized with well-placed borders and shading.
Activate the Borders sheet	On this worksheet, the same data has no borders or shading and does not appear as organized.
2 Select A5:G17	
Click as shown	
	(The Borders button is on the Formatting toolbar.) The Borders palette appears.
Select the indicated border	
	To apply a Thick Box Border to the selected range.

3 Deselect the range	To view the border you have applied.
4 Select A5:G5	You'll apply Thick Bottom Border to the selected range.
Display the Borders palette	
Select the indicated border	

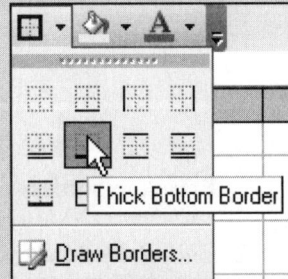

(Display the Borders palette.) To apply the Thick Bottom Border to the selected range.

Deselect the range	
5 Select A5:A17	
Apply the indicated border	

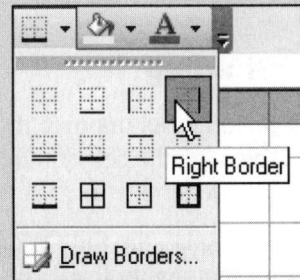

(Display the Borders palette.) To apply a border to the right edge of the selected range.

6 Apply a right border to B5:B17	(Select the range, and select Right Border from the Borders palette.)
7 Apply a left border to G5:G17	(Select the range, and select Left Border from the Borders palette.)
8 Apply the Thick Box Border to A11:G11 and A17:G17	(Select the first range, press Ctrl, and select the second range.)
9 Apply the Thick Bottom Border to C2:E2 and B3:F3	
Deselect the range	
10 Compare the **Borders** and **Sales** worksheets	The Borders sheet has an extra border below "Outlander Spices."

11	Activate the Borders sheet	(If necessary.)
	Choose **Format**, **Erase Border**	The pointer changes to an eraser. You'll remove the extra border below "Outlander Spices."
	Click as shown	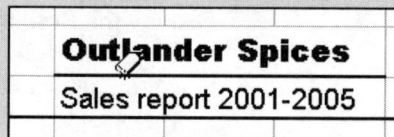
		To erase the border from C2.
	Erase the borders from D2 and E2	
12	Choose **Format, Cells...**	To open the Format Cells dialog box.
	Activate the Border tab	More border options are available in the Border tab than in the Borders palette.
	Click **OK**	To close the Format Cells dialog box.
13	Update the workbook	

Shading

Explanation

Shading can improve the visual appeal of a worksheet. You can add shading by selecting the cell or range you want to apply shading to and selecting a color from the Fill Color palette.

To display the Fill Color palette, click the arrow next to the Fill Color button on the Formatting toolbar. You can also apply shading by using the Patterns tab in the Format Cells dialog box.

Do it! **A-2: Adding shading to a cell or range**

Here's how	Here's why
1 Select A5:G5	You'll apply different shades to distinguish the different ranges.
Click as shown	(The Fill Color button is on the Formatting toolbar.) The Fill Color palette appears. The color name will appear as a ToolTip when you point to a color on the palette.
Select as shown	
Deselect the range	To view the shading you applied to A5:G5.
2 Select A6:A10 and A12:A16	(Select the first range, press Ctrl, and select the second range.)
From the Fill Color palette, select as shown	
3 Apply Gray-25% shading to C2:E2	
4 Apply Aqua shading to G6:G10 and G12:G16	
5 Apply Pale Blue shading to A11:G11, A17:G17, and B3:F3	
6 Compare the **Borders** and **Sales** worksheets	The worksheets have the same formatting. However, the colors might differ.
7 Update the workbook	

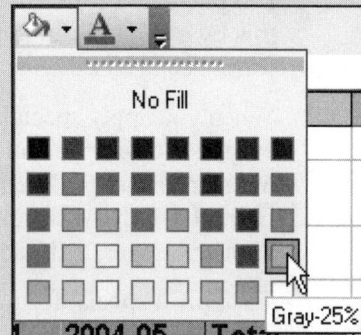

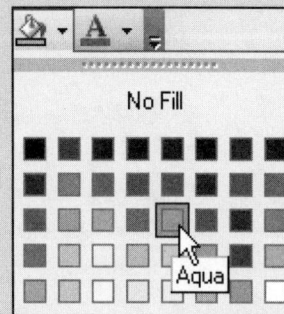

Topic B: Using special number formats

This topic covers the following Microsoft Office Specialist exam objective.

#	Objective
XL03E-2-1	Creating and applying custom number formats

Special number formats

Explanation

You can apply special number formats—such as ZIP codes, Social Security numbers, and phone numbers— to change the appearance of numerical information. You can do this by using built-in formats or by creating your own custom formats. You can also format cells based on conditions.

When you apply special number formats to the data in your worksheets, Excel changes only the cell's appearance and not the cell's value. So, when you click a cell in which a number format has been applied, the formula bar still displays the unformatted value. Exhibit 4-1 shows a worksheet to which special number formats, such as Zip Code, Phone Number, and Social Security Number, have been applied.

To apply a special format:

1   In the Format Cells dialog box, activate the Number tab.

2   From the Category list, select Special.

3   From the Type list, select a format type. Click OK.

City	Zip code	Name	SSN	Phone number
Ashford	06278	Bill MacArthur	421-11-1111	(907) 345-4024
Georgetown	80444	Jamie Morrison	467-20-9932	(800) 228-1425
Elbert	80106	Maureen O'Connor	534-98-7549	(520) 284-0767
Farmington	06032	Rebecca Austin	816-17-3312	(635) 565-4581
North Franklin	06254	Paul Anderson	631-10-3178	(357) 613-2978
North Grosvenordale	06255	Cynthia Roberts	133-30-3389	(526) 563-2440
North Windham	06256	Rita Greg	332-20-1728	(246) 344-6657
Elizabeth	80107	Trevor Johnson	376-31-3383	(545) 454-5457
Franktown	80116	Kevin Meyers	225-51-2998	(632) 653-5235
Bennett	80102	Adam Long	336-68-4467	(677) 376-3760
Quinebaug	06262	Kendra James	712-35-4665	(327) 587-6636
Rogers	06263	Michael Lee	189-85-3313	(523) 436-6373
Scotland	06264	Sandra Lawrence	193-30-3331	(527) 786-7872
South Willington	06265	Mary Smith	389-10-2721	(633) 646-4643
South Windham	06266	James Overmire	213-44-4548	(545) 865-6544
South Woodstock	06267	Annie Philips	172-41-0712	(774) 777-4383
Stonington	06378	Shannon Lee	212-21-2232	(567) 575-8787
Storrs Mansfield	06268	Roger Williams	312-71-3816	(245) 767-6432
Thompson	06277	Melissa James	372-16-2728	(347) 676-8857

Exhibit 4-1: The Number formats worksheet with special formats applied

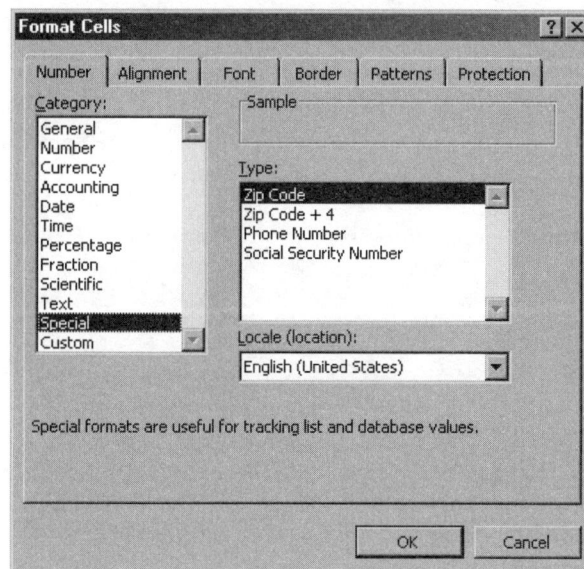

Exhibit 4-2: The Number tab in the Format Cells dialog box

B-1: Using special formats

Here's how	Here's why
1 Activate the Number formats sheet	This worksheet contains the award details for managers.
2 Select B5:B23	The Zip code column contains four- and five-digit ZIP codes. You'll apply the Zip Code format to this range to make sure that all ZIP codes contain five digits.
3 Choose **Format**, **Cells...**	To open the Format Cells dialog box.
Activate the Number tab	
From the Category list, select **Special**	The Special category includes formats for ZIP codes, phone numbers, and Social Security numbers. In the Type list, Zip Code is selected, as shown in Exhibit 4-2.
Click **OK**	
Deselect the cells	The ZIP code values have been reformatted. Each four-digit ZIP code now begins with zero.
4 Select D5:D23	You'll apply the Social Security Number format to these values.
5 Open the Format Cells dialog box	(Choose Format, Cells. The Number tab is active.)
From the Category list, select **Special**	
From the Type list, select **Social Security Number**	
Click **OK**	To apply the Social Security Number format to the selected range.
6 Select D5	421111111
	The formula bar still displays the unformatted value because Excel changes only the appearance of the value in the cell and not the cell value itself.

7	Apply the Phone Number format to E5:E23	(Use the Format Cells dialog box.)
8	Select E5	
	Observe the formula bar	9073454024
		The cell value remains the same even though you have changed its display format in the worksheet.
9	Update the workbook	

Zero values

Explanation

Excel displays all zero values in a worksheet by default. However, if you prefer, you can hide zero values. To do so:

1 Choose Tools, Options.
2 Activate the View tab in the Options dialog box.
3 Under Window options, clear Zero values.
4 Click OK.

Do it!

B-2: Controlling the display of zero values

Here's how	Here's why
1 Verify that the Number formats sheet is active	The Excellence awards and Gold medals columns contain several zero values.
2 Open the Options dialog box	(Choose Tools, Options.)
Activate the View tab	(If necessary.)
Under Window options, clear **Zero values**	
Click **OK**	The cells that contained zero values earlier are now blank.
3 Update the workbook	

Custom number formats

Explanation

In Excel, you can create custom formats in which you specify the appearance of positive numbers, negative numbers, zero values, and text data.

To create a custom number format, activate the Number tab in the Format Cells dialog box. From the Category list, select a Custom category. Then, in the Type box, enter the format code. Click OK to apply the format.

A custom format code contains four sections—positives, negatives, zeros, and text—separated by semicolons. The syntax for all format codes is:

```
positive;negative;zero;text
```

The first section specifies how a positive value will appear in a cell. In the negative section, you can specify how a negative value should appear in a cell. You can use the zero section to control the display of zero values, and use the text section to control the appearance of text data in a cell. You can skip a section by entering consecutive semicolons.

Here's an example:

```
#,###.00_);[Red](#,###.00);0.00;"text"@
```

The # and 0 (zero) symbols are placeholders for digits. You can specify how a numeric value should appear in a cell by using these symbols. The code #,###.00 in the positive section of the example means that positive numbers should have a comma in every thousandths position and two digits after the decimal point.

The underscore (_) adds a space equal to the size of the character following it to the value in the cell. In the example, negative numbers are enclosed in parentheses. The underscore in the positive section is followed by a closing parenthesis so that the positive numbers line up correctly with negative numbers. In the negative section, [Red] indicates that all negative values will appear in the color red. The at symbol (@) displays a text value in a cell. You can identify specific text to be added automatically at the beginning of a text value by enclosing that text in double quotes before the @ symbol. Exhibit 4-3 shows the effects of some of these format codes.

Name	City	SSN	Gold medals	Sales (2003-04)	Sales (2004-2005)	% Increase
Bill MacArthur	Ashford	SSN-421-11-1111	1	$ 67,678.00	$135,567.00	100.31
Jamie Morrison	Georgetown	SSN-467-20-9932		$ 76,576.00	$ 65,737.00	(14.15)
Jim Adams	Elbert	SSN-534-98-7549		$ 114,867.00	$114,688.00	(0.16)
Rebecca Austin	Farmington	SSN-816-17-3312		$ 76,357.00	$ 86,548.00	13.35
Paul Anderson	North Franklin	SSN-631-10-3178		$ 85,566.00	$ 89,076.00	4.10
Cynthia Roberts	North Grosvenordale	SSN-133-30-3389		$ 39,076.00	$ 56,546.00	44.71
Rita Greg	North Windham	SSN-332-20-1728		$ 78,678.00	$ 67,888.00	(13.71)
Trevor Johnson	Elizabeth	SSN-376-31-3383		$ 64,874.00	$ 87,688.00	35.17
Kevin Meyers	Franktown	SSN-225-51-2998	3	$ 85,559.00	$184,888.00	116.09
Adam Long	Bennett	SSN-336-68-4467		$ 75,770.00	$ 85,665.00	13.06
Kendra James	Quinebaug	SSN-712-35-4665		$ 65,578.00	$ 55,786.00	(14.93)
Michael Lee	Rogers	SSN-189-85-3313		$ 69,867.00	$ 78,798.00	12.78
Sandra Lawrence	Scotland	SSN-193-30-3331	1	$ 76,377.00	$129,867.00	70.03
Mary Smith	South Willington	SSN-389-10-2721		$ 75,786.00	$ 98,566.00	30.06
James Overmire	South Windham	SSN-213-44-4548		$ 56,587.00	$ 78,979.00	39.57
Annie Philips	South Woodstock	SSN-172-41-0712		$ 78,698.00	$ 65,789.00	(16.40)
Shannon Lee	Stonington	SSN-212-21-2232		$ 68,985.00	$ 89,089.00	29.14
Roger Williams	Storrs Mansfield	SSN-312-71-3816		$ 75,677.00	$ 87,588.00	15.74
Melissa James	Thompson	SSN-372-16-2728	1	$ 85,386.00	$ 10,984.00	(87.14)

Exhibit 4-3: The Custom format worksheet after custom formats have been applied

Do it!

B-3:   Creating custom formats

Here's how	Here's why
1 Activate the Custom format sheet	This sheet contains the 2004–2005 performance details for managers. Notice that the values in the % Increase column are difficult to interpret.
2 Select G5:G23	These cells contain positive and negative values.
Open the Format Cells dialog box	The Number tab is active.
3 From the Category list, select **Custom**	To display the types of Custom formats.
From the Type list, select **#,##0.00_);[Red](#,##0.00)**	
Click **OK**	The values in the % Increase column are rounded to the hundredths place. Excel rounds the values up or down as necessary. Negative values appear in red.
4 Select D5:D23	You'll hide the zeros in the Gold medals column.
Open the Format Cells dialog box	
From the Category list, select **Custom**	
Edit the Type box to read **0;-0;;@**	(This format is not in the Type list, so you must enter it in the Type box.) Here, ";;" indicates that the zeros section in the format code is empty; therefore, zeros will not be displayed. The @ symbol specifies that the cells in the range can accept and display text values.
Click **OK**	The cells containing zero values are now blank.
5 Select C5:C23	You'll add a prefix to all the values in this column, identifying them as Social Security numbers.
Open the Format Cells dialog box	
From the Category list, select **Custom**	000-00-0000 is the default selection.
6 Edit the Type box to read **"SSN-"000-00-0000**	
Click **OK**	The prefix "SSN-" appears before all values in the SSN column.
7 Update the workbook	

Conditional formatting

Explanation

Formatting that is applied to data only if a specific condition is satisfied is called *conditional formatting*. You can highlight the values satisfying a specific condition in a different color or format. For example, you can highlight all the sales figures that exceed $100,000 in yellow. To apply conditional formatting to cells, use the Conditional Formatting dialog box. Conditional formatting can be applied based on a cell value or a formula. You can specify up to three format conditions per cell.

To apply conditional formatting based on cell values:

1   Select the cells to which you want to apply the formatting.
2   Choose Format, Conditional Formatting to open the Conditional Formatting dialog box.
3   From the first list, select Cell Value Is to format cells based on their values.
4   From the second list, select an operation.
5   Enter the required values in the text boxes.
6   Click the Format button to open the Format Cells dialog box.
7   In the Format Cells dialog box, specify the format in which the cells satisfying the condition should appear, and click OK.
8   Click OK to apply the format.

To apply conditional formatting based on formulas:

1   Select the cells to which you want to apply the formatting.
2   Choose Format, Conditional Formatting to open the Conditional Formatting dialog box.
3   From the first list, select Formula Is to format cells based on a formula.
4   In the text box, enter a formula that evaluates a value to be True or False.
5   Click the Format button to open the Format Cells dialog box.
6   In the Format Cells dialog box, specify the format in which the cells satisfying the condition should appear, and click OK.
7   Click OK to apply the format.

Do it!

B-4:   Applying conditional formatting

Here's how	Here's why
1 Select E5:F23	You'll apply formatting to sales figures exceeding $75,000.
2 Choose **Format, Conditional Formatting...**	To open the Conditional Formatting dialog box.
3 In the first list, verify that "Cell Value Is" is selected	To format the cells based on the cell values.

4 From the second list, select **greater than**, as shown

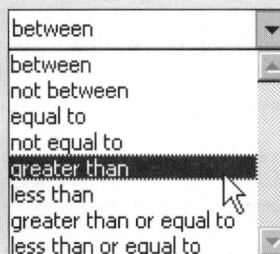

> between ▼
>
> | between |
> | not between |
> | equal to |
> | not equal to |
> | **greater than** |
> | less than |
> | greater than or equal to |
> | less than or equal to |

To check whether the cell value is greater than a specified value.

5 In the third text box, enter the value **75000**

6 Click **Format**

(The Format button is in the Conditional Formatting dialog box.) To open the Format Cells dialog box.

7 Verify that the Font tab is active

8 From the Color list, select as shown

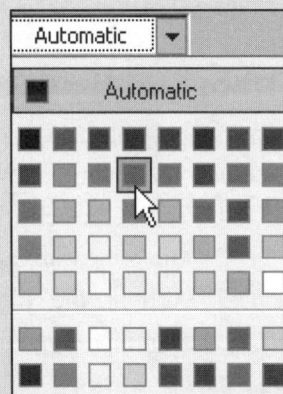

> Automatic ▼
>
> ■ Automatic

To apply a green color to the formatted values.

9 Click **OK**

To close the Format Cells dialog box and return to the Conditional Formatting dialog box.

10 Click **OK**

To close the Conditional Formatting dialog box.

11 Deselect the cells

The cells with values more than $75,000 appear in green.

12 Update the workbook

Topic C: Working with dates

This topic covers the following Microsoft Office Specialist exam objective.

#	Objective
XL03S-2-4	Creating formulas using the following function categories: Statistical, Date and Time, Financial, and Logical (e.g., Sum, Min, Max, Date or Now, PMT, IF, Average) (This objective is also covered in *Excel 2003: Basic*, in the unit titled "Using functions," as well as in *Excel 2003: Advanced*, in the unit titled "Working with advanced formulas.")

How Excel stores date information

Explanation

Excel provides various formats to display the date and time. You can also perform calculations based on date and time values. This is possible because Excel stores dates as serial numbers. Date values begin at 01/01/1900, which Excel interprets as serial number 1. For every day past this date, Excel adds 1 to the serial number. For example, the serial number for 01/08/2005 is 38360 because January 8, 2005, is 38,360 days past January 1, 1900.

Date and time formats

You can view date and time values in several formats. Date and time formats can include year, month, day, and time in various styles. To apply a date format:

1 Select the cells that you want to apply the date format to.

2 Open the Format Cells dialog box.

3 Activate the Number tab. From the Category list, select Date.

4 From the Type list, select a date format. Click OK.

Product	Sample code	Date of testing	Sample date & time	Expiry date
Cinnamon (Ground Korintje)	ST657	13-May-03	5/14/03 0:00	November 13, 2006
Cinnamon (Ground) Extra High Oil (2X)	ST647	23-Jun-03	6/23/03 13:00	December 23, 2004
Anise Seeds	ST499	21-Sep-03	9/22/03 9:00	March 21, 2004
Annatto Seed	ST819	12-Jul-03	7/13/03 11:30	January 12, 2004
Asafoetida Powder	ST325	19-Aug-03	8/19/03 19:40	February 19, 2004
Basil Leaf (Whole)	ST300	26-Mar-03	3/26/03 21:00	September 26, 2005
Basil Leaf (Ground)	ST014	22-Jun-03	6/23/03 14:00	December 22, 2005
Cardamom Seed (Ground)	ST304	31-Mar-03	4/1/03 14:00	September 30, 2004
Carob Powder (Raw)	ST417	21-Apr-03	4/22/03 0:00	October 21, 2006
Carob Pods (Ribbled)	ST668	29-Jan-03	1/31/03 15:45	July 29, 2006

Exhibit 4-4: The Dates worksheet with date formats applied

Do it!

C-1: Using date and time formats

Here's how	Here's why
1 Activate the Dates sheet	This worksheet contains product-sample test details.
2 Select C5:C14	This is the Date of testing column.
Open the Format Cells dialog box	The Number tab is active. In the Category list, Date is selected by default.
From the Type list, select **14-Mar-01**	The date will appear in this format.
Click **OK**	The dates appear in a format that shows the day, an abbreviation of the month, and a two-digit year.
3 Select D5:D14	This is the Sample date & time column.
Open the Format Cells dialog box	
From the Category list, select **Date**	
From the Type list, select **3/14/01 13:30**	(Scroll down, if necessary.)
Click **OK**	This format includes the date and time in a 24-hour format.
4 Apply the March 14, 2001 format to E5:E14	
5 Update the workbook	The worksheet should look like Exhibit 4-4.

Date functions

Explanation

You can use Excel's date functions to analyze and calculate date values. For example, you might have a column of expiration dates that need to be calculated based on today's date. These calculations can be done with date functions.

The NOW function

The NOW function inserts the serial number of the current system date and time. The syntax for the NOW function is:

```
NOW()
```

The NOW function updates the current date and time each time you perform calculations on the data and whenever you run a macro containing this function. It does not automatically change the value in the cell with the system time.

The DATE function

The DATE function inserts the serial number for the date based on the arguments passed to the function. The syntax for the DATE function is:

```
DATE(year,month,day)
```

If the year argument is between 0 and 1899, Excel adds the specified number to 1900 to calculate the year. If the month argument is greater than 12, Excel adds the specified number of months to the first month of the specified year. If the day argument is greater than the number of days in the specified month, Excel adds the specified number of days to the first day of the specified month.

Do it!

C-2: Using the NOW and DATE functions

Here's how	Here's why
1 Select F5	You'll use the NOW function to enter the current date and time.
Enter **=NOW()**	A serial number appears, indicating the current date and time. This value will change automatically over the course of the activities.
Apply the 3/14/01 1:30 PM date format to F5	
2 Copy the formula in F5 to F6:F14	The current date and time appear in all cells in this column.
Apply the Thick Bottom Border to F14	(The border disappeared when the formula was copied to the cell.)
3 Select G5:G14	You'll use the DATE function to specify the next inspection date for all products in the worksheet.
Apply the March 14, 2001 date format	After you apply the format, the cells remain blank because you have not entered any values or functions yet.

4 In G5, enter
   =DATE(2005,3,1)

In this formula, 2005 refers to the year 2005, 3 refers to the third month of the year (March), and 1 refers to the first day of the month. Because the year argument (2005) is greater than 1899, the DATE function uses this number as the year value without performing any year calculations. The formatted date March 1, 2005 appears in the cell.

5 In G6, enter
   =DATE(105,3,1)

This formula is different from the previous one but will yield the same result. Because the year argument (105) is less than 1899, the DATE function adds this number to 1900 to calculate the year value. March 1, 2005 appears in this cell as well.

6 In G7, enter
   =DATE(2004,15,1)

This formula is different from the previous two but again will yield the same result. In this formula, the month value (15) is greater than 12, so the DATE function adds this number to the first month of the specified year (2004). In other words, Excel will calculate the month and year by adding 15 months to January 2004. The value March 1, 2005, which is 15 months past January 2004, appears in G7.

   Copy the formula in G7 to
   G8:G14

   Apply the Thick Bottom Border to
   G14

7 Update the workbook

Calculations on dates

Explanation
You can use dates in calculations because Excel stores dates as serial numbers. For example, you can calculate the number of days between two dates or calculate a date that is a certain number of days after another date. You can also calculate the number of months between two dates, or the number of years between two dates.

To find the difference between two dates, use the subtraction operator (-) just as you would to find the difference between any two numbers.

Do it!

C-3: Performing calculations on dates

Here's how	Here's why
1 Activate the Date calculations sheet	
2 Select D5	You'll calculate the expiration date for the ST657 sample.
Enter **=C5+1000**	To calculate the date that is 1,000 days after the date in C5.
Observe D5	06-Feb-06
	You can see the date 1,000 days after the date in D5.
3 Copy the formula in D5 to D6:D14	To calculate the expiration dates for the remaining samples.
4 Select E5	You'll calculate the number of days remaining for the ST657 sample to expire.
Enter **=D5-NOW()**	This formula subtracts the current date from the date in D5. The ST657 sample expires in this number of days.
5 Copy the formula in E5 to E6:E14	To calculate the number of days remaining before the samples expires.
6 Calculate all dates of next inspection (column G) by adding 100 days to the dates of last inspection (column F)	(If you need a hint, see Steps 2 and 3.) The date of next inspection for all products is March 10, 2004.
Apply the Thick Bottom Border to cells D14, E14, and G14	
7 Update the workbook	

Topic D: Working with styles

This topic covers the following Microsoft Office Specialist exam objective.

#	Objective
XL03S-3-2	Applying styles (e.g., applying a style from the Format>Style list)

What's a style?

Explanation

You might want to apply several formatting options at the same time. Applying them individually would be time consuming. You can do this efficiently by creating a style that has all the formatting options you want to apply, and then applying that style to the worksheet. A *style* is a collection of formats that are saved and applied as a group.

Excel provides several built-in styles. You can also create and modify your own styles to make data appear exactly as you want.

Built-in styles

You can view the built-in styles by choosing Format, Style to open the Style dialog box and clicking the Style name arrow. When you select a style from the Style name list, a series of checked boxes appears, indicating the formatting options associated with that style.

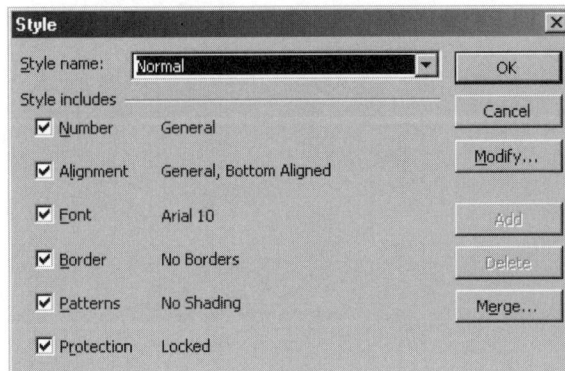

Exhibit 4-5: The Style dialog box

Do it!

D-1: Observing built-in styles

Here's how	Here's why
1 Choose **Format**, **Style...**	To open the Style dialog box, as shown in Exhibit 4-5. By default, Normal is selected in the Style name box. Under Style includes, the checked options indicate the formatting options included in the Normal style.
2 Click as shown	Normal ▼ Comma Comma [0] Currency Currency [0] Followed Hyperlink Hyperlink **Normal** Percent To display the list of eight built-in styles.
3 Select **Comma**	Notice that only the Number check box is checked in the dialog box.
4 Click **Cancel**	To close the Style dialog box without applying a style.

Custom styles

Explanation

You can also create your own styles that combine formatting in any way you want. To create a custom style:

1 Select a cell that already has the combination of formats you want to include in the new style.

2 Choose Format, Style to open the Style dialog box.

3 In the Style name box, enter the name of the new style.

4 Click OK to define the new style.

You apply a defined style (built-in or custom) by selecting the cell(s) you want to apply the style to and selecting a style from the Style name box in the Style dialog box. Whether you use a built-in or custom style, the procedures for applying and modifying these styles are the same.

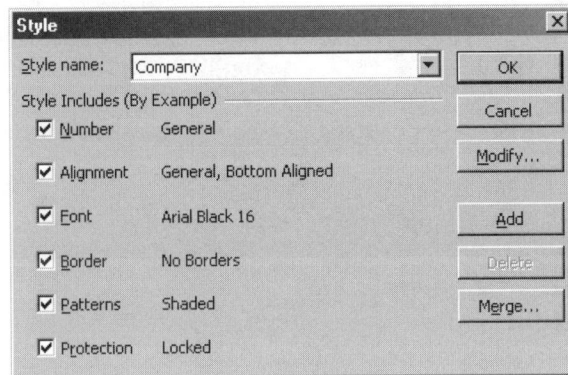

Exhibit 4-6: The Style dialog box showing the new style Company

D-2:   Creating and applying styles

Here's how	Here's why
1 Activate the Custom format sheet	
2 Select A1	(If necessary.) You'll create a new style based on the format of A1.
Open the Style dialog box	(Choose Format, Style.)
Edit the Style name box to read **Company**	(As shown in Exhibit 4-6.) To name the new style. Under Style Includes (By Example), the formatting options of the new style are checked. These match the formatting options of the selected cell (A1).
Click **OK**	To create a new style called Company, which you'll apply to the Styles worksheet.
3 Select G6	You'll create a new style based on the format of G6.
Open the Style dialog box	
In the Style name box, type **NegativeNum**	
Under Style Includes (By Example), clear **Border**	To ensure that the style, when applied, does not alter the borders of the target cell(s).
Click **OK**	To create a new style called NegativeNum, which you'll apply to the Styles worksheet.
4 Create a style named **Column heading** based on A4	(Select the cell, open the Style dialog box, enter Column heading in the Style name box, and then click OK.)
5 Create a style named **Title** based on A2	
6 Activate the Styles sheet	You'll apply the styles you created to the data in this worksheet.
Select A1:C1	
Open the Style dialog box	
From the Style name list, select **Company**	
Click **OK**	To apply the new style to the selected range. A1:C1 has been reformatted to the style Company.

7 Apply the Title style to A2:C2

8 Apply the Column heading style
   to A4:E4

9 Apply the NegativeNum style to   The new styles you created are applied to the
   E5:E23   data in the Styles worksheet.

10 Update the workbook

Modifying styles

Explanation

To modify a style (built-in or custom):

1 In the Style dialog box, select the name of the style you want to modify.
2 Click Modify to open the Format Cells dialog box.
3 Select the formats you want to add to (or remove from) the style.
4 Click OK to close the Format Cells dialog box.
5 Click OK to close the Style dialog box.

Do it!

D-3: Modifying styles

Here's how	Here's why
1 Select E5	(If necessary.)
2 Open the Style dialog box	(Choose Format, Style.) You'll modify the NegativeNum style you created earlier.
From the Style name list, select **NegativeNum**	(If necessary.) Under Style includes, the checked boxes indicate the formatting options that make up this custom style.
Click **Modify**	To open the Format Cells dialog box. You can use this dialog box to modify any defined style (built-in or custom).
3 Under Category, select **Number**	(On the Number tab.) If necessary.
Edit the Decimal places box to read **1**	To specify that values displayed with the NegativeNum style will have only one digit to the right of the decimal point.
From the Negative numbers list, select **-1234.0**	To specify that negative values displayed with the NegativeNum style will appear in black, preceded by a minus (-) sign.
Click **OK**	To close the Format Cells dialog box and return to the Style dialog box.
Click **OK**	

% Increase
100.3
-14.2
-0.2
13.3
4.1
44.7
-13.7
35.2

The % Increase column displays the values according to the modified NegativeNum style. All decimals are rounded to the tenths place, and negative numbers appear in black, preceded by a minus (-) sign.

4 Update the workbook

Topic E: Other advanced formatting

Explanation

You can improve the appearance of text in a worksheet by giving it a more arranged look. You can merge cells, center cells, and use indents to align text within cells or within text boxes.

Merging cells in a worksheet

You can center text that extends across multiple cells by merging those cells into one. To do this, select the cells to be merged, and in the Format Cells dialog box, on the Alignment tab, check Merge cells. You can merge cells in a column or a row. After the cells have been merged, you can use alignment options to change the position of the text within the merged cell. You can split the cells by clearing the Merge cells check box.

Merging and centering

When you want to merge cells and center the text within the merged cell horizontally, you use the Merge and Center button on the Formatting toolbar. You can change the horizontal and vertical alignment of text by using the Alignment tab in the Format Cells dialog box.

Indenting text in a merged cell

Another alignment option that you can use for text within merged cells is indents. You can indent text from the left by specifying a value in the Indent box on the Alignment tab in the Format Cells dialog box. The value in the Horizontal alignment box will change to reflect a left indent.

Do it!

E-1: Merging cells

Here's how	Here's why
1 Activate the Sales sheet	You'll insert a table title in this worksheet.
2 Insert a new column before column A	(Select column A, right-click, and choose Insert from the shortcut menu.) An Insert Options smart tag appears.
3 Select A5 Enter **East and North regions**	The text is not completely visible.
4 Select A5:A17 Click [Merge and Center icon]	(The Merge and Center button is on the Formatting toolbar.) The cells have been merged into one cell, but the text is still not completely visible. The text appears at the bottom of the cell.
5 Update the workbook	

Cell orientation

Explanation

You can change a cell's orientation to display text differently. *Cell orientation* refers to the direction of text flow in a cell. By default, text appears horizontally. You can also display it vertically or rotate it to a specific angle.

To do this, you use the Orientation box on the Alignment tab in the Format Cells dialog box. You can specify a value between 0 and 90 degrees for the text orientation by using the Degrees box. A preview of the angle is displayed for you.

In addition to changing the orientation, you can change the vertical alignment of the text in the cell by using the Vertical alignment options.

Product	Region	2001-2002	2002-2003	2003-2004	2004-2005
Cinnamon (Ground Korintje)	East	$20,345	$29,196	$17,990	$18,158
Cinnamon (Ground) Extra High Oil (2X)	East	$26,400	$34,879	$15,541	$22,731
Anise Seeds	East	$2,253	$2,139	$11,312	$20,218
Annatto Seed	East	$2,146	$1,871	$11,771	$24,181
Asafoetida Powder	East	$18,772	$18,780	$19,426	$23,273
Sub total (East)		$69,916	$86,865	$76,039	$108,561
Basil Leaf (Whole)	North	$2,511	$2,158	$17,611	$25,166
Basil Leaf (Ground)	North	$3,829	$1,753	$17,314	$17,924
Cardamom Seed (Ground)	North	$3,190	$2,471	$17,975	$25,573
Carob Powder (Raw)	North	$3,248	$3,253	$13,839	$18,336
Carob Pods (Ribbled)	North	$2,301	$2,468	$17,648	$23,818
Sub total (North)		$15,079	$12,103	$84,388	$110,817

(Row label on left side: *East and North regions*)

Exhibit 4-7: A sample of the Sales worksheet after Step 3

Do it!

E-2:   Changing a cell's orientation

Here's how	Here's why
1 Select A5	(If necessary.) You'll change the orientation of text within the cell so that the title is completely visible.
2 Open the Format Cells dialog box	
Activate the Alignment tab	A preview of the orientation appears in the Orientation box, which is set horizontally at the default value of 0 degrees.
Edit the Degrees box to read **90**	To specify that the text be rotated 90 degrees.
Under Text alignment, from the Vertical list, select **Center**	
Click **OK**	To apply the changes.
3 Click [**B**]	(The Bold button is on the Formatting toolbar.) To make the text bold. The text in A5 is displayed vertically, centered in the merged cell, and bold, as shown in Exhibit 4-7.
4 Update the workbook	

Splitting merged cells

Explanation

After you have merged a range of cells, you might need to split them. To do so, select the cells, and clear Merge cells on the Alignment tab in the Format Cells dialog box. You can also use the Merge and Center button to merge or split cells.

Do it!

E-3:   Splitting cells

Here's how	Here's why
1 Activate the Split cells sheet	This worksheet contains the sales report for four salespersons. The table title is merged and centered across the five columns containing the sales report. You'll add the sales details for a fifth salesperson, and then split the cells containing the table title so that it extends over all six columns.
In F4, enter **Tina Ralls**	To enter the name of the fifth salesperson.
In F5:F8, enter data as shown	$4,600 $5,200 $4,900 $1,550
2 Apply borders to the new column of data so that this column matches the other columns	
3 Select A3	The range A3:E3 gets selected because the cells in this range are merged.
Click [icon]	(The Merge and Center button is on the Formatting toolbar.) To split the cells in the range A3:E3.
4 Select A3:F3	You'll merge and center the table title across the new range.
Click [icon]	The table title is merged and centered across all six columns.
5 Update and close the workbook	

Unit summary: Advanced formatting

Topic A   In this topic, you learned how to add **borders** to a cell or range by using the **Borders palette**. You also learned how to add **shading** by using the **Fill Color palette**.

Topic B   In this topic, you learned how to apply **special number formats** to ZIP codes, Social Security numbers, and phone numbers. You learned how to hide or display **zero values** in an entire worksheet and in a selected range. You learned how to use **custom formats** to display data in specific formats. You also learned how to apply **conditional formatting** to cells.

Topic C   In this topic, you learned how to apply **date** and **time formats**. You used the **NOW function** to insert the current date and time, and the **DATE function** to insert specific dates. You also learned how to perform calculations based on date values.

Topic D   In this topic, you learned about the **built-in styles** that Excel provides. You learned how to **create** and **apply new styles**. You also learned how to **modify styles**.

Topic E   In this topic, you learned how to **merge cells**, use **indents** to align text within cells, change the **orientation** of text within cells, and **split** merged cells.

Independent practice activity

1 Open Practice advanced formatting (from the current unit folder), and save it as **My practice advanced formatting**. Verify that the Practice advanced formatting sheet is active.

2 Apply a Thick Box border to A4:E20.

3 Apply a Thick Bottom border to A4:E4.

4 Apply Tan shading to A1:E1, Lime shading to A2:E2, and 40% Gray shading to A4:E4.

5 Apply Aqua shading to B5:B20, and Pale Blue shading to E5:E20.

6 Apply the built-in Social Security Number format to C5:C20.

7 Apply the March 14, 2001 format to D5:D20.

8 Calculate the contract end dates for all employees. Contract end dates are 365 days after their respective contract start dates.

9 Compare your worksheet with Exhibit 4-8.

10 Create custom styles called **Company**, **Title**, **Column heading**, **Names**, and **Contract end dates** based on the current worksheet. Apply these styles to the Apply styles worksheet.

11 Merge and center the company name and the subtitle over the entire width of the data.

12 Update the workbook and close it.

Outlander Spices				
Employee contract details				
Employee code	Name	SSN	Contract start date	Contract end date
E025	Pamela Carter	421-11-1111	May 13, 2003	May 12, 2004
E026	Anna Morris	467-20-9932	June 23, 2003	June 22, 2004
E027	Rita Lawson	534-98-7549	September 21, 2003	September 20, 2004
E028	Sam Peters	816-17-3312	July 12, 2003	July 11, 2004
E029	Julie George	631-10-3178	August 19, 2003	August 18, 2004
E030	Diana Stone	133-30-3389	March 26, 2003	March 25, 2004
E031	Rob Dukes	332-20-1728	June 22, 2003	June 21, 2004
E032	Tammy Heiret	376-31-3383	March 31, 2003	March 30, 2004
E033	Sandy Stewart	225-51-2998	April 21, 2003	April 20, 2004
E034	Wendy Alto	336-68-4467	January 29, 2003	January 29, 2004
E035	Tina Ralls	712-35-4665	May 13, 2003	May 12, 2004
E036	Nikki Cleary	189-85-3313	June 23, 2003	June 22, 2004
E037	Davis Lee	193-30-3331	September 21, 2003	September 20, 2004
E038	David Ford	389-10-2721	July 12, 2003	July 11, 2004
E039	Julia Stockton	213-44-4548	August 19, 2003	August 18, 2004

Exhibit 4-8: A sample of the My practice advance formatting worksheet after Step 8

Review questions

1 List the steps you can use to apply a special number format.

2 When you apply special number formats to the data in a worksheet, Excel changes both the cell's appearance and the cell's value. True or False?

3 What is conditional formatting?

4 Which function updates the current date and time each time you perform calculations on the data?

5 What is a style?

Unit 5

List management

Unit time: 35 minutes

Complete this unit, and you'll know how to:

A Use lists to organize data logically.

B Sort lists by the contents of their columns, and filter lists to show only those rows that meet certain criteria.

C Use the Custom AutoFilter and Advanced Filter dialog boxes to filter lists based on complex criteria.

Topic A: Examining lists

Explanation

You can create lists in your worksheets to organize data in a concise and logical format. A *list* is a series of rows containing related data.

Structure of a list

A list is made up of records, fields, and field names. *Records* are simply the rows of data in a list. *Fields* are the columns of data in a list. *Field names* are the column headings, which appear in the first row of the list. A sample Excel list is shown in Exhibit 5-1.

	A	B	C	D	E	F	
1	**Employee information**						
2							
3	**Name**	**Emp code**	**SSN**	**Region**	**Department**	**Earning ($)**	⎯ Field name
4	Diana Stone	30	372-12-7281	East	Marketing	60000	
5	Jesse Bennet	23	284-78-9701	South	Sales	250500	
6	Rita Greg	9	612-20-9800	East	Sales	380050	
7	Adam Long	18	640-62-8586	North	Administration	90000	⎯ Record
8	Anna Morris	26	312-13-8162	West	Accounts	150000	
9	Annie Philips	6	553-06-2429	West	Human resources	60000	
10	David Ford	38	631-10-1786	North	Customer support	150200	
11	Davis Lee	37	467-29-9320	East	Accounts	73500	
12	James Overmire	4	283-18-6190	South	Marketing	105000	⎯ Field
13	Jamie Morrison	19	201-90-1901	East	Human resources	62000	
14	Julia Stockton	39	332-21-7283	West	Customer support	96600	
15	Kevin Meyers	17	712-35-6656	West	Accounts	84000	

Exhibit 5-1: The structure of a list

Do it!

A-1: Examining the structure of a list

Here's how	Here's why
1 Open Employee information	(From the current unit folder.) You'll examine the structure of the Employee information in Sheet1 of this workbook.
Save the workbook as **My employee information**	In the current unit folder.
2 Observe A3:F3	The column headings in this range are the field names for this list.
3 Observe A5:F5	This row represents one record. In this list, each record contains all the related information for an individual employee: Name, Emp code, SSN, Region, Department, and Earning ($).
4 Observe A4:F43	Each cell represents a field value for a specific record.

Topic B: Sorting and filtering lists

This topic covers the following Microsoft Office Specialist exam objectives.

#	Objective
XL03S-2-1	Filtering lists using AutoFilter
XL03S-2-2	Sorting lists

Sorting lists

Explanation

Sorting refers to organizing the data in a list in ascending or descending order by the contents of one or more columns in the list.

To sort a list, select any cell in the column by which you want to sort. Then, on the Standard toolbar, click the Sort Ascending or Sort Descending button. This will sort the entire list, including all records, not just the column containing the selected cell.

Do it!

B-1: Sorting a list by using the Standard toolbar

Here's how	Here's why
1 Select B4	You'll sort the rows of employee information by the contents of this column, Emp code, in ascending order. You can select any cell in the column by which you want to sort.
2 Click [A/Z↓]	

Name	Emp code
Malcolm Pingault	1
Shannon Lee	2
Melinda McGregor	3
James Overmire	4
Roger Williams	5
Annie Philips	6

(The Sort Ascending button is on the Standard toolbar.) The rows are now organized in ascending order by employee code.

3 Update the workbook

Sorting lists based on two or more columns

Explanation   You can also sort a list based on data in two or more columns. For example, you can sort employee information by Region and Department, as shown in Exhibit 5-2. In this case, all the employees in a single region are grouped together and then sorted by department.

Employee information					
Name	**Emp code**	**SSN**	**Region**	**Department**	**Earning ($)**
Melissa James	7	423-82-1129	East	Accounts	87000
Davis Lee	37	467-29-9320	East	Accounts	73500
Wendy Alto	34	111-90-2730	East	Administration	105000
Sonia McCormick	40	187-01-9192	East	Administration	78000
Roger Williams	5	265-66-9763	East	Customer support	90000
Malcolm Pingault	1	133-30-3891	East	Human resources	72000
Paul Anderson	11	189-85-3133	East	Human resources	180000
Jamie Morrison	19	201-90-1901	East	Human resources	62000
Diana Stone	30	372-12-7281	East	Marketing	60000
Sandy Stewart	33	816-13-3129	East	Marketing	65000
Rita Greg	9	612-20-9800	East	Sales	380050
Kendra James	16	101-12-9111	East	Sales	144000
Sandra Lawrence	15	213-44-5487	North	Accounts	100000
Mary Smith	8	193-33-3314	North	Administration	104000
Adam Long	18	640-62-8586	North	Administration	90000
Stuart Young	22	876-07-1750	North	Customer support	94000
David Ford	38	631-10-1786	North	Customer support	150200

Exhibit 5-2: The Employee information list sorted by Region and Department

To sort a list based on two or more columns:

1   Select any cell in the list.

2   Choose Data, Sort to open the Sort dialog box.

3   From the Sort by list, select the column heading of the column by which you want to sort the list, and then select a sorting order. All records will be sorted first based on the column and the sorting order you selected.

4   From the Then by list, select the column and order by which you want to sort rows.

5   Click OK.

Do it!   **B-2:   Sorting a list by using the Sort command**

Here's how	Here's why
1 Select any cell in the list	
2 Choose **Data**, **Sort...**	

(Sort dialog box shown with: Sort by "Emp code" Ascending; Then by (two) Ascending; My list has Header row / No header row; Options..., OK, Cancel)

To open the Sort dialog box.

Under Sort by, from the list, select **Region**	To specify that the list be sorted first by region.
Under Sort by, verify that Ascending is selected	The list will be sorted by region in ascending or alphabetical order.
3 From the first Then by list, select **Department**	When rows have the same value in the Region column, they will be sorted by department. The default order is Ascending.
Click **OK**	To display the sorted list in the worksheet. All the employees in a region are now grouped together, beginning with the East region. For each region, the department names are sorted in ascending alphabetical order, as shown in Exhibit 5-2.
4 Update the workbook	

Filtering lists

Explanation

You can *filter* a list when you want to display only those rows of information that meet specific criteria. To help you do this, Excel provides the AutoFilter feature. Here's how it works:

1   Select any cell in the list.

2   Choose Data, Filter, AutoFilter to display the AutoFilter arrows next to each column heading.

3   From the list for the column by which you want to filter, select a criterion.

To show the entire list again, choose Data, Filter, Show All.

Do it!

B-3:   Filtering a list by using AutoFilter

Here's how	Here's why
1 Select any cell in the list	(If necessary.)
Choose **Data**, **Filter**, **AutoFilter**	\[Name ▾\] \[Emp cod ▾\] The AutoFilter arrows appear to the right of all the column headings.
2 Click the AutoFilter arrow next to Department	**Department** ▾ Sort Ascending Sort Descending (All) (Top 10...) (Custom...) Accounts Administraion Administration Customer support Human resources Marketing Sales To display a list of filter criteria from which you can choose.
Select **Accounts**	To display only the records of employees in the Accounts department. All other records are hidden.
3 From the Region list, select **West**	To display only the records of those employees in the Accounts department who work in the West region.
4 Choose **Data**, **Filter**, **Show All**	To display the complete, unfiltered list.
5 Choose **Data**, **Filter**, **AutoFilter**	To turn off the AutoFilter feature. The AutoFilter arrows next to the column headings disappear.

Topic C: Advanced filtering

This topic covers the following Microsoft Office Specialist exam objectives.

#	Objective
XL03E-1-2	Creating and applying advanced filters
XL03E-1-5	Creating and modifying list ranges

Filtering tools

Explanation

You can filter a list based on more than one criterion by using Excel's advanced filtering features. For example, you can display the records of all those employees whose department is either Marketing or Sales. Excel provides two tools for specifying multiple filter criteria:

- Custom AutoFilter
- Advanced Filter

Custom AutoFilter

You can use the Custom AutoFilter dialog box to specify more than one criterion for the same column heading.

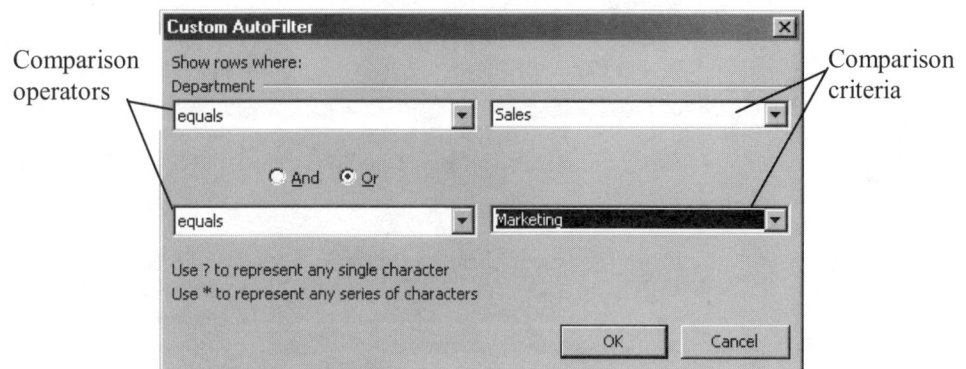

Comparison operators

Comparison criteria

Exhibit 5-3: The Custom AutoFilter dialog box

In Exhibit 5-3, Department is the column for which custom criteria have been created. The first criterion states that the department must be Sales; the second criterion states that the department must be Marketing. The two criteria are joined by the Or operator, meaning that rows will be included in the filtered list if they meet *either* criterion. When you use the And operator, the rows must meet *both* criteria. The criteria in Exhibit 5-3 would yield a list of employees in either the Sales department or the Marketing department.

To filter a list by using the Custom AutoFilter dialog box:

1 Turn on AutoFilter for the list.

2 From the drop-down list of the column for which you want to create criteria, choose Custom to display the Custom AutoFilter dialog box.

3 Select the first comparison operator and its associated comparison criterion.

4 Select And or Or. By selecting And, you'll decrease the number of rows that meet the criteria. By selecting Or, you'll increase the number of matching rows.

5 Select the second comparison operator and its associated comparison criterion. Click OK.

Do it!

C-1: Using the Custom AutoFilter criteria

Here's how	Here's why
1 Select E4	You'll display the records of those employees who belong to either the Sales or the Marketing department.
2 Choose **Data**, **Filter**, **AutoFilter**	To turn on AutoFilter. The AutoFilter arrows appear next to the column headings.
3 From the Department list, select **(Custom...)**	To open the Custom AutoFilter dialog box. In the upper-left list, the first comparison operator, equals, is selected.
From the upper-right list, select **Sales**	To specify the first comparison criterion.
Select **Or**	This tells Excel to display all records that match either of the two comparison criteria.
4 From the lower-left list, select **equals**	To specify the second comparison operator.
From the lower-right list, select **Marketing**	To specify the second comparison criterion. The Custom AutoFilter dialog box now resembles Exhibit 5-3.
Click **OK**	The worksheet displays records of employees who work in either the Sales or the Marketing department.
5 Choose **Data**, **Filter**, **AutoFilter**	To turn off AutoFilter. The worksheet displays the unfiltered list.

Creating a criteria range

Explanation

In some cases, you might want to filter records based on two or more column headings with multiple criteria. For example, you might want to display the records of all East region employees whose salaries are greater than $100,000 and all West region employees whose salaries are greater than or equal to $80,000. You can use a criteria range to filter data based on such complex criteria.

A *criteria range* is a cell range containing a set of search conditions. It consists of one row of criteria labels and at least one row that defines the search conditions. The criteria label must be the name of a column for which you want to specify a criterion. To filter a list according to a criteria range, you use the Advanced Filter dialog box.

The following table lists the comparison operators that you can use in a criteria range:

Operator	Meaning
=	Equal to
>	Greater than
<	Less than
>=	Greater than or equal to
<=	Less than or equal to
<>	Not equal to

To create a criteria range by using the Advanced Filter dialog box:

1 Enter at least one criteria label in a cell that is *not* adjacent to the range that contains the list. The criteria label must be exactly the same as the column heading in the list.

2 Enter a comparison criterion below the cell that contains the criteria label.

3 Choose Data, Filter, Advanced Filter to open the Advanced Filter dialog box.

4 In the List range box, enter the cell range you want to filter. The cell range must include the associated column headings.

5 In the Criteria range box, enter the cell range that contains your criteria.

6 Click OK.

C-2: Using the Advanced Filter dialog box

Here's how	Here's why
1 In H3, enter **Region**	To specify the first criteria label. Ensure that the criteria label matches the column heading in the list exactly. Copying and pasting the column headings is a good way to ensure that the labels are identical to those in the list.
In I3, enter **Earning ($)**	To specify the second criteria label. Be sure to include the space between Earning and ($).
2 In H4, enter **East**	To specify East as the first comparison criterion.
In I4, enter **>100000**	To complete the first row of criteria. This criterion will display only those values in the East region that have earnings greater than $100,000.
3 In H5, enter **West**	To specify West as the second criterion.
In I5, enter **>=80000**	(The second row of the criteria range will display values in the West region that have earnings greater than or equal to $80,000.) Adding rows to a criteria range amounts to using an Or operator, so rows will be included if they meet either of these conditions.
4 Select any cell in the list	You'll enter the entire list range automatically when you choose the Advanced Filter command.
Choose **Data**, **Filter**, **Advanced Filter...**	To open the Advanced Filter dialog box. "Filter the list, in-place" is selected by default. This means that the filtered list will be displayed in the same worksheet. The entire list appears selected in the worksheet.
5 Click ▣	(The Collapse dialog button is in the Advanced Filter dialog box, next to the Criteria range box.) The Advanced Filter – Criteria range: dialog box appears.
Select H3:I5	To enter the criteria range.

6 Click 🖾

Advanced Filter	✕
Action	
● Filter the list, in-place	
○ Copy to another location	
List range:	$A$3:$F$43 🖳
Criteria range:	Sheet1!$H$3:$I$5 🖳
Copy to:	🖳
☐ Unique records only	
	OK Cancel

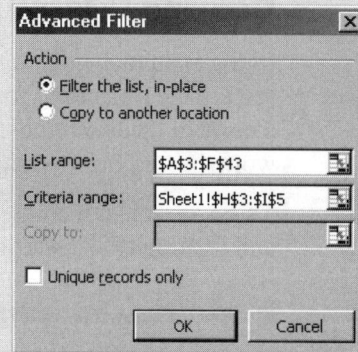

(The Collapse dialog button is in the Advanced Filter – Criteria range: dialog box.) To expand the Advanced Filter – Criteria range: dialog box.

Click **OK**

The list now displays the records of the employees in the East region whose salaries are greater than $100,000, as well as the employees in the West region whose salaries are greater than or equal to $80,000.

7 Display the unfiltered list

(Choose Data, Filter, Show All.)

8 Update the workbook

Copying filtered results to another location

Explanation

In the examples you've seen so far, rows are filtered out of the list so that all you can see are the remaining rows. You can also choose to keep the original list intact and place a copy of the filtered list somewhere else within the same worksheet or in another worksheet in the workbook.

To do so, select the Copy to another location option in the Advanced Filter dialog box, and then specify a starting cell for the copied list.

Do it!

C-3:   Copying filtered results to another range

Here's how	Here's why
1 Open the Advanced Filter dialog box	(Choose Data, Filter, Advanced Filter.) The list and criteria ranges that were previously entered in the dialog box are still there.
2 Select **Copy to another location**	
Click 🔲	The Collapse dialog button is in the Advanced Filter dialog box, next to the Copy to box.
Select H10	This cell will be the starting point for the filtered result list.
3 Click 🔲	

Advanced Filter dialog box:
- Action
  - ○ Filter the list, in-place
  - ● Copy to another location
- List range: $A$3:$F$43
- Criteria range: $H$3:$I$5
- Copy to: Sheet1!$H$10
- ☐ Unique records only
- OK   Cancel

Click **OK**	The worksheet displays the filtered list in the specified location.
4 Update and close the workbook	

Unit summary: List management

Topic A
In this topic, you learned about the structure of a **list**. You learned that a list displays related data in a concise and logical manner. You also learned that a list is made up of field names, fields, and records. You learned that the rows in a list are called **records** and the columns are called **fields**. You also learned that **field names** are the column headings that appear in the first row of a list.

Topic B
In this topic, you learned how to **sort** a list by the data in one or more of its columns. You learned that you can sort a list in ascending or descending order based on the values in a column. You also learned how to use the **AutoFilter** feature to **filter** a list to show only those rows that meet certain criteria.

Topic C
In this topic, you learned how to use the **Custom AutoFilter** dialog box to filter a list based on multiple criteria. You learned how to use a **criteria range** and the **Advanced Filter** command to specify more complex criteria. You also learned how to copy a filtered list to another location.

Independent practice activity

1 Open Practice list, and save it as **My practice list**.

2 Sort the list by Product code in ascending order.

3 Sort the list first by Re-order level (Kg) in descending order, and then by Product name in ascending order.

4 Use AutoFilter to display only those records for the supplier Cedric Stone. Then, display all records again.

5 Display only those records for the suppliers Cedric Stone or Bill Johnson. Then, display all records again.

6 Create a filtered list to display only those records where the re-order level is greater than 2,000 and less than 3,500. (*Hint:* Use Custom AutoFilter.)

7 Compare your result with Exhibit 5-4.

8 Turn off AutoFilter.

9 Use the criteria labels in F2:G2 to create a criteria range to display only those records where the re-order level for Cedric Stone is greater than 2,000 or the re-order level for Bill Johnson is greater than 3,000. Copy the filtered result to a different location in the worksheet so that you can view the filtered and unfiltered lists simultaneously.

10 Compare your results with Exhibit 5-5.

11 Update and close the workbook.

	A	B	C	D
1	**Product info**			
2	Product name ▾	Product code ▾	Suppliers ▾	Re-order level(K ▾
13	Basil leaf (ground)	20	Richie Hamond	3200
14	Caraway seed (ground)	14	Bill Johnson	3200
15	Cardamom seed (whole)	8	Anthony Felix	3000
16	Chives	31	Paul Michelin	3000
17	Cinnamon (ground) extra high oil (2x)	12	Anthony Felix	3000
18	Catnip leaf	26	Charles Nought	2900
19	Anise seeds	18	Bill Johnson	2800
20	Coarse kosher salt flakes	36	Henry Sanders	2800
21	Cassia	2	Garry Harper	2600
22	Anise	32	Cedric Stone	2500
23	Chinese star anise (whole)	27	Dennis Linekar	2500
24	Celery seed (ground)	12	Andy Howard	2300
25	Caraway seed (whole)	16	Michael Smith	2100
26	Cloves (whole)	35	Charly Bobbit	2100

Exhibit 5-4: A sample of the My practice list worksheet after Step 6

Product name	Product code	Suppliers	Re-order level(Kg)
Cardamom seed (ground)	5	Cedric Stone	4000
Caraway seed (ground)	14	Bill Johnson	3200
Anise	32	Cedric Stone	2500

Exhibit 5-5: A sample of the My practice list worksheet after Step 9

Review questions

1 What is a list?

2 List the steps you would use to sort a list.

3 What menu choice will display the AutoFilter arrows next to each column heading?

4 What is a criteria range?

5 List the steps you would use to keep an original list intact and place a copy of the filtered list somewhere else within the same worksheet.

Unit 6

Advanced charting

Unit time: 30 minutes

Complete this unit, and you'll know how to:

A Adjust the scale of a chart, and format data points.

B Create combination charts and trendlines to highlight different kinds of data.

C Add and format graphic elements to highlight a specific portion of a chart, and add a picture to a worksheet.

Topic A: Chart formatting options

Explanation

Excel provides many formatting options for charts. You can use these options to represent or interpret complex data. For example, you can change the scale of an entire chart or format specific data points.

Adjusting the scale of a chart

You can change the scale of a chart to:

- Adjust the range of values on each axis.
- Change the way the values appear on each axis.
- Specify the intervals at which the values appear.
- Set the point at which one axis crosses another.

To change the scale of a chart, select the value axis and display the Chart toolbar. On the Chart toolbar, click the Format button to open the Format Axis dialog box. Activate the Scale tab, as shown in Exhibit 6-1. The following table summarizes the options available on the Scale tab:

Option	Description
Minimum	Specifies the lowest value on the value axis.
Maximum	Specifies the highest value on the value axis.
Major unit	Specifies the intervals for major tick marks and major gridlines on the value axis.
Minor unit	Specifies the intervals for minor tick marks and minor gridlines on the value axis.
Category (X) axis	Specifies the point at which the category axis crosses the value axis.

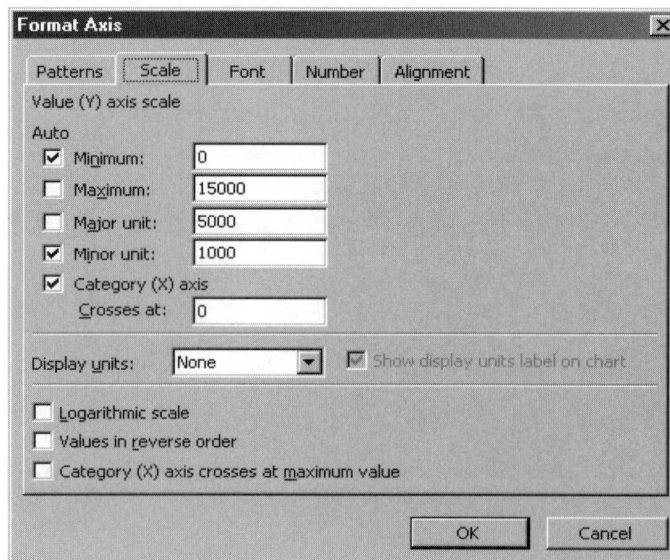

Exhibit 6-1: The Scale tab in the Format Axis dialog box

Do it!   **A-1:   Adjusting the scale of a chart**

Here's how	Here's why
1 Open Charts	From the current unit folder.
Save the workbook as **My charts**	In the current unit folder.
Verify that the Scale sheet is active	
	The Scale sheet contains the quarterly sales report for five Outlander Spices salespeople. On the chart, the value axis displays a minimum value of 0 and a maximum value of 15,000. The interval between the values is 5,000. This scale is not suitable because the value axis is too large, making the columns seem small and minimizing the difference between data points.
2 Select the value axis	The Chart toolbar appears. In the Chart Objects list, Value Axis is selected. You'll change the scale of the value axis.
Click	(The Format button is on the Chart toolbar.) To open the Format Axis dialog box.
Click the **Scale** tab	You'll change the scale options.
3 Edit the Maximum box to read **10000**	
Edit the Major unit box to read **2000**	
Click **OK**	
	To close the Format Axis dialog box and apply the new scale options. The value axis now displays a minimum value of 0 and a maximum value of 10,000. The major tick marks occur at intervals of 2,000. This scale is more appropriate for the data.
4 Update the workbook	

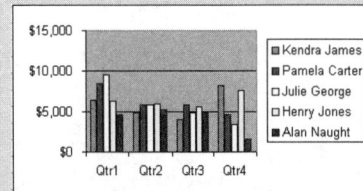

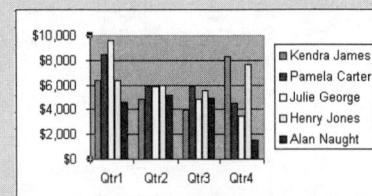

Formatting data points

Explanation

You can change the appearance of data points to make them stand out or make them easier to understand. You can add or remove labels, percentages, or leader lines. A *leader line* is a line from the data label to its associated data point. In a pie chart, you can change the orientation of the first slice or pull out a slice to make it stand out.

Labeling a data point

To add a label to a data point:

1 Select the data point you want to label.
2 Choose Format, Selected Data Point to open the Format Data Point dialog box.
3 Activate the Data Labels tab.
4 Select a label option, and click OK.

Pulling out a slice in a pie chart

You can pull out a slice in a pie chart by dragging it away from the pie. This helps you draw attention to a specific data point.

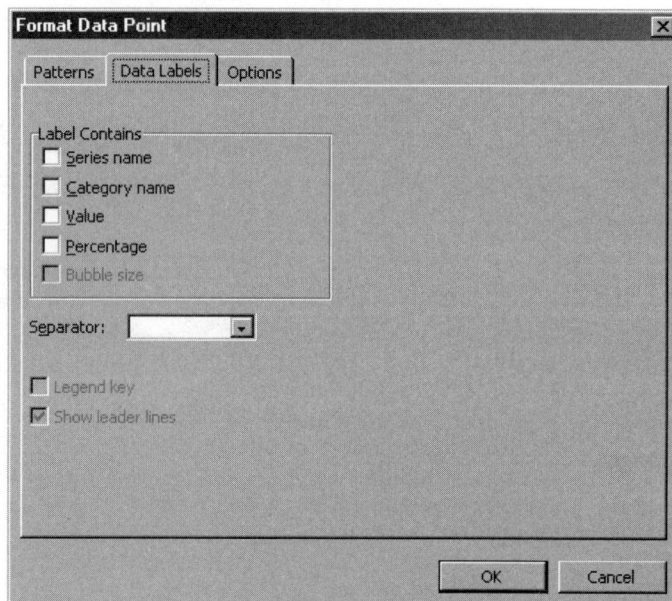

Exhibit 6-2: The Data Labels tab in the Format Data Point dialog box

Do it!

A-2: Formatting a data point

Here's how	Here's why
1 Activate the Datapoint sheet	This worksheet contains the total yearly sales report for several products. The pie chart represents a breakdown of sales by product.
2 Select the slice representing cinnamon sales	(Click the pie, and then click the slice.) You'll add a label to this data point.
Click 🖾	(The Format button is on the Chart toolbar.) To open the Format Data Point dialog box.
Activate the Data Labels tab	As shown in Exhibit 6-2.
3 Under Label Contains, check **Percentage**	
Click **OK**	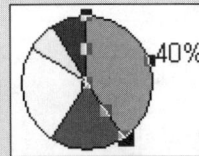 To display a percentage value next to the selected Cinnamon data point.
4 Drag the selected slice slightly to the right	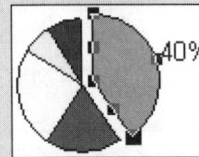 To pull out the slice for cinnamon sales away from other slices. This will make the Cinnamon data point stand out from the other data points.
5 Update the workbook	

Topic B: Using combination charts

Explanation

You can combine two or more chart types in a single chart, called a *combination chart*. For example, you can combine a column chart with a line chart. Other combinations of charts are also possible. You can use combination charts when you want to represent a wider range of information or when you want to highlight a series or the contrast between different series. You can also graphically represent variations in data by using trendlines.

Creating combination charts

At times, you might need to show two kinds of information on the same chart. For example, in Exhibit 6-3, the columns show expense and sales figures, measured in thousands of dollars, while the line shows profit figures, which are percentages. You can create combination charts either by selecting that overall chart type or by applying a secondary axis to one or more series within a chart.

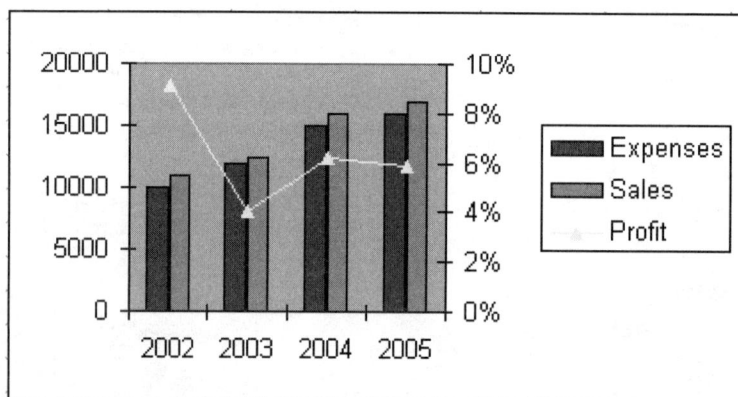

Exhibit 6-3: A sample column-line combination chart

To create a combination chart by changing the chart type:

1 Select the chart.

2 Choose Chart, Chart Type to open the Chart Type dialog box.

3 Activate the Custom Types tab. From the Chart type list, select a type that includes two type names.

4 Click OK.

To create a combination chart that uses a secondary value axis:

1 Display the Format Data Series dialog box for the series you want to plot on a secondary axis.

2 Activate the Axis tab, and select Secondary axis.

3 Click OK.

Do it!   **B-1:   Creating a combination chart**

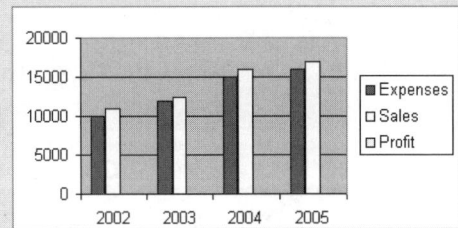

Here's how	Here's why
1 Activate the Combination sheet	
	This sheet displays profit trends from 2002 to 2005. On the chart, the category axis represents the years, and the value axis represents the sales. Profit is not visible on the chart because the Profit values are too small relative to the Expenses and Sales values.
2 Select the chart	
From the Chart Objects list, select **Series "Profit"**	(The Chart Objects list is on the left end of the Chart toolbar.) You'll create a secondary value axis to represent the Profit data series.
Click	(The Format button is on the Chart toolbar.) To open the Format Data Series dialog box.
3 Click the **Axis** tab	
Select **Secondary axis**	
Click **OK**	
	The secondary axis appears on the right side of the chart. The Profit data series overlaps the other two data series.

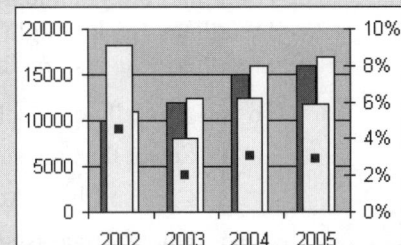

4 Choose **Chart**, **Chart Type...**	To open the Chart Type dialog box. The Standard Types tab is activated. You'll change the chart type to line-column, in which the Profit data series will be represented as a line.
Click the **Custom Types** tab	
From the Chart type list, select **Line – Column on 2 Axes**	(You might have to scroll down to view the option.)
Click **OK**	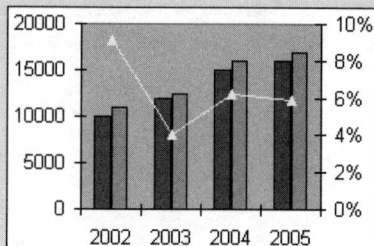
	To change the chart type for the Profit data series from column to line. Now it's easier to understand how profit percentage fluctuates with respect to expenses and sales.
5 Update the workbook	

Creating trendlines

Explanation

You can create trendlines in charts to emphasize the patterns of change in your data. *Trendlines* are graphical representations of drifts or variations in a data series. Trendlines can highlight important variations and make your charts easier to understand. Trendlines can also facilitate prediction and decision making.

To add a trendline to a chart:

1. Select the data series to which you want to add a trendline.
2. Choose Chart, Add Trendline to open the Add Trendline dialog box.
3. Under Trend/Regression type, select a trendline.
4. Click OK.

Do it!   **B-2:   Creating a trendline**

Here's how	Here's why
1 Activate the Trendline sheet	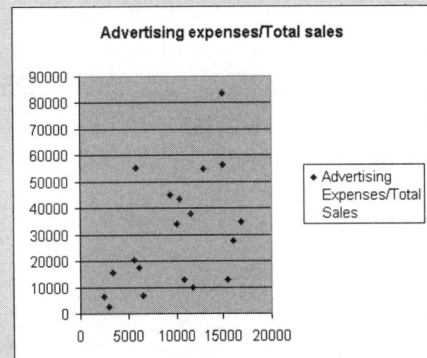
This worksheet shows the advertising expenses and total sales for the years 1987–2005. From the chart, it's difficult to determine whether sales increase or decrease relative to changes in advertising expenses.
2 Select the chart	You'll create a trendline for the Advertising Expenses/Total Sales data series.
3 Choose **Chart**, **Add Trendline...**	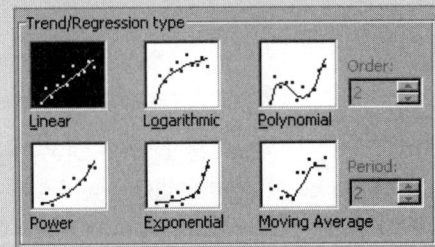
(To open the Add Trendline dialog box.) The Linear trendline is selected by default.
4 Click **OK**	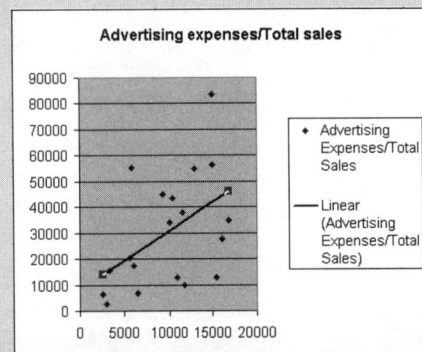
(To display the trendline on the chart.) The trendline indicates that total sales increase with increase in advertising expenses.
5 Update the workbook	

Topic C: Using graphic elements

This topic covers the following Microsoft Office Specialist exam objectives.

#	Objective
XL03S-1-4	Inserting, positioning, and sizing graphics
XL03S-2-5	Creating, modifying, and positioning diagrams and charts based on data contained in the active workbook (This objective is also covered in *Excel 2003: Basic*, in the unit titled "Creating charts.")
XL03E-2-3	Format and resize graphics
	• Using cropping and rotating tools
	• Controlling image contrast and brightness
	• Scaling and resizing graphics

Why should I use graphic elements?

Explanation

You can highlight a specific portion of a chart by adding graphic elements, such as text boxes, lines, and arrows. You can also format these elements to make them stand out or fit in better.

The Drawing toolbar

You can use the Drawing toolbar to create lines, arrows, text boxes, shapes, and 3-D graphic objects in the chart area. To create an object by using the Drawing toolbar, click the button for the shape you want, point to where you want the shape to begin, and drag to create the shape.

Do it!   ## C-1: Adding graphic elements

Here's how	Here's why
1 Activate the Graphic sheet	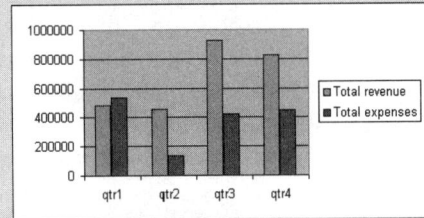
	This worksheet contains a chart of quarterly revenue and expenses for all four quarters. You'll add graphic elements to enhance the chart.
2 Display the Drawing toolbar	(Choose View, Toolbars, Drawing.)
Click	(The Text Box button is on the Drawing toolbar.) You'll add a text box to the chart.
Drag as shown	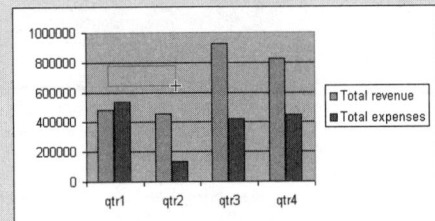
	To create a text box in the plot area of the chart.
3 Type **Sales hike**	(In the text box.) You'll emphasize the steep rise in sales in the third quarter.
Click outside the chart area	To deselect the text box, so that you can see it on the chart.
4 Click	(The Arrow button is on the Drawing toolbar.) The pointer takes the shape of a crosshair that you can use to draw an arrow.
Point to the upper-right corner of the text box	The foot of the arrow will be here.
Drag as shown	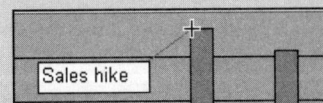
	To create an arrow pointing from the text box to the tallest column of the chart. The text and the arrow emphasize the steep rise in sales.
Click outside the chart area	
5 Update the workbook	

Formatting graphic elements

Explanation

You can change the shape, size, or color of graphic elements by using their Format dialog boxes, which have different names depending on the element selected. You can display these dialog boxes by double-clicking an element. You can also format the text in a text box just as you would format text in a cell. Exhibit 6-4 shows the Format AutoShape dialog box, which you can use to format autoshapes.

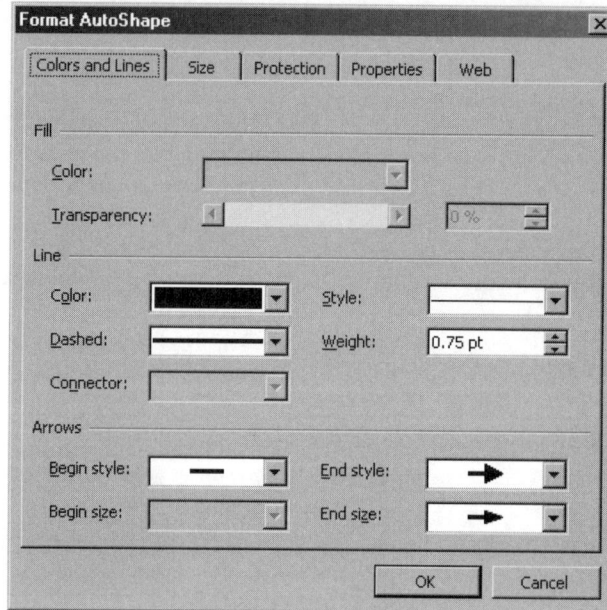

Exhibit 6-4: The Format AutoShape dialog box

The following table describes the tabs of the Format AutoShape dialog box:

Tab	Use this tab to...
Colors and Lines	Specify line styles, arrow styles, and colors for fills and lines.
Size	Specify the size and rotation of the selected object.
Protection	Prevent users from modifying or copying the selected object.
Properties	Specify whether resizing the chart will affect the size of the selected graphic object and whether the graphic object will be printed when you print the worksheet.
Web	Specify the text that should appear while you load pictures on the Web or in browsers that do not support graphics.

Do it!   ## C-2:   Formatting a graphic element

Here's how	Here's why
1 Double-click the Sales hike arrow	The Format AutoShape dialog box opens with the Colors and Lines tab activated by default.
2 From the End style list, select as shown	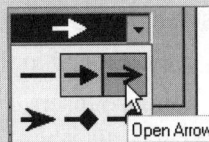 To apply a different style for the arrowhead.
From the Style list, select as shown	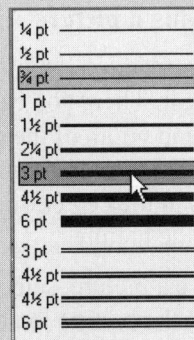
Click **OK**	To apply the changes.
3 Select the text box	(Click the border of the text box.)
Click **B**	(The Bold button is on the Formatting toolbar.) To make the text bold. You might need to resize the text box so that all the text is visible.
4 Deselect the text box	(Click outside the chart.)
5 Update the workbook	

Working with pictures

Explanation

You might want to include a picture on a worksheet to emphasize a specific point or to add some humor. You can insert pictures from the Clip Organizer or from a file. After you have inserted a picture, you can move, resize, and delete it just as you would any other object.

To insert a picture from a file:

1   Select a cell in the worksheet.
2   Choose Insert, Picture, From File to open the Insert Picture dialog box.
3   Open the folder that contains the picture.
4   Select the picture, and click Insert.

Modifying a picture

You can resize and move a picture. To resize a picture, you must first select it by clicking it. Then, you can drag the corner sizing handles to increase or decrease the height and width of the picture at the same time. *Sizing handles* are the small squares or circles that appear around the border of the picture when it's selected. You can use the handles in the center of each side to increase or decrease the height or width of a single side of the picture.

To move a picture, select it and drag it to a new location on the worksheet. If you want to move the picture to another worksheet or workbook, use the Edit, Cut command.

You can use the buttons on the Picture toolbar to rotate or crop a picture. You can also rotate a picture by dragging the rotate handle on the picture in the direction in which you want to rotate it. Any picture in Excel can be cropped, except for an animated GIF.

You can also adjust a picture's brightness and contrast. To increase or decrease the brightness of a picture, use the More Brightness or Less Brightness buttons on the Picture toolbar. To increase or decrease the contrast, use the More Contrast or Less Contrast buttons.

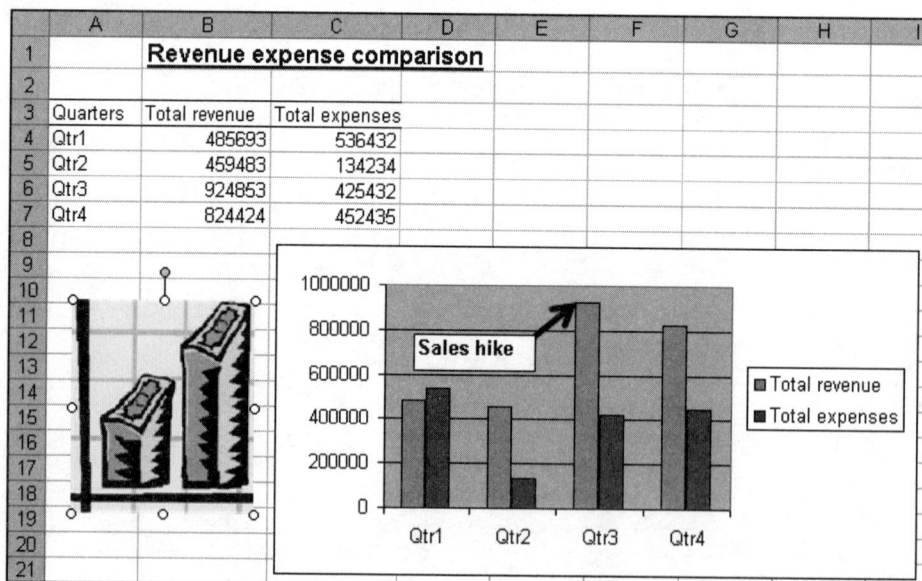

Exhibit 6-5: The Graphic worksheet with a picture inserted in it

Do it!

C-3: Adding a picture to a worksheet

Here's how	Here's why
1 Select C24	You'll insert a picture here.
2 Choose **Insert**, **Picture**, **From File...**	To open the Insert Picture dialog box.
3 Navigate to the current unit folder	
Select **Profit**	You'll insert this picture into the worksheet.
Click **Insert**	(You might need to scroll to view the picture.) To insert the picture, Profit. The Picture toolbar appears. The picture is large, so you'll crop and resize it.
4 Click [crop icon]	(The Crop button is on the Picture toolbar.) Cropping handles appear around the picture.
5 Point to the cropping handle on the lower-right corner of the picture, and drag as shown	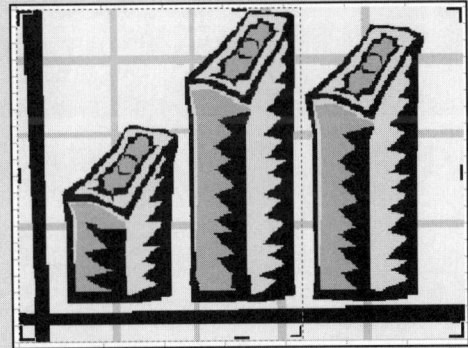
	To remove the third bar.
Press ESC	The sizing handles appear around the cropped picture.
6 Point to the sizing handle on the lower-right corner of the picture, and resize the picture as shown	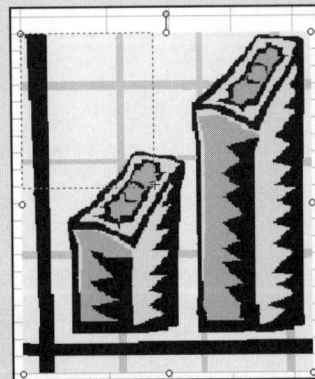
	To resize the picture proportionately.
7 Drag the picture to the left of the chart	As shown in Exhibit 6-5. The picture is now positioned to the left of the chart.

8 Click [icon] twice	(The More Brightness button is located on the Picture toolbar.) To increase the brightness of the picture.
Click [icon] twice	(The Less Brightness button is located on the Picture toolbar.) To decrease the brightness of the picture.
9 Click [icon] twice	(The More Contrast button is located on the Picture toolbar.) To increase the contrast in the picture.
Click [icon] twice	(The Less Contrast button is located on the Picture toolbar.) To decrease the contrast in the picture.
Deselect the picture	(Click any blank cell.) To close the Picture toolbar.
10 Update and close the workbook	

Unit summary: Advanced charting

Topic A   In this topic, you learned how to **adjust** the **scale** of a chart. You also learned how to **format data points** by **adding data labels**. You learned that you can add data labels, such as the percentage value of a data point, to the chart. You also learned how to **pull out** a slice in a pie chart.

Topic B   In this topic, you learned how to **create** a **combination chart** by using two value axes. You also learned how to **add trendlines** to a chart, and you learned that they can be used to highlight the variations of data in a data series.

Topic C   In this topic, you learned how to **add** and **format graphic elements** in a chart. You learned that graphic elements can be used to emphasize a specific point in a chart. You also learned how to **add** a **picture** to a worksheet.

Independent practice activity

1 Open Practice charts, and save it as **My practice charts**.

2 Activate the Column worksheet.

3 Change the maximum scale value of the value axis to 250.

4 Add a text box to the chart, and enter **Lowest sales** as shown in Exhibit 6-6.

5 Add an arrow from the text box to the column showing the lowest sales.

6 Compare your chart with Exhibit 6-6.

7 Create a linear trendline for the data in the Trend worksheet.

8 Create a combination chart for the data in the Combination worksheet. (*Hint:* Select the Profit Trend chart. From the Chart Objects list, select Series "Profit." Choose Chart, Chart Type. On the Custom Types tab, select Line – Column on 2 Axes from the Chart Type list. Click OK.)

9 Update and close the workbook.

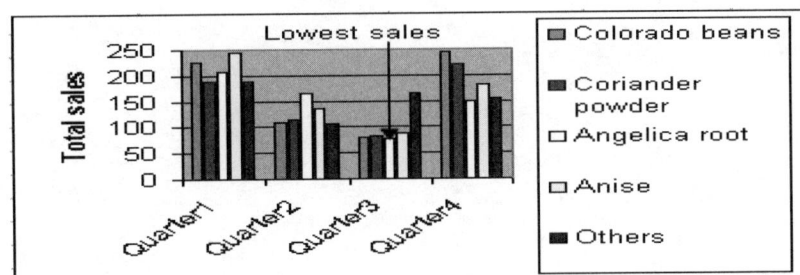

Exhibit 6-6: The chart after Step 5

Review questions

1 What is a leader line?

2 What is a combination chart?

3 List the steps you would use to insert a picture from a file.

4 What are sizing handles?

5 What command would you use to move a picture from one workbook to another?

Unit 7
Documenting and auditing

Unit time: 60 minutes

Complete this unit, and you'll know how to:

A Use auditing features to trace precedent and dependent cells, and trace errors.

B Add comments and text boxes to a worksheet.

C Protect a worksheet or part of a worksheet against unauthorized access or unintentional changes.

D Share workbooks, merge versions of a workbook, and track changes by various users.

Topic A: Auditing features

This topic covers the following Microsoft Office Specialist exam objectives.

#	Objective
XL03E-1-11	Trace formula precedents, dependents and errors
	• Tracing formula precedents
	• Tracing formula dependents
	• Tracing formula errors
XL03E-1-12	Using Error Checking

Dependent and precedent cells

Explanation

You might want to identify the cells on which the value of a formula is based. Excel provides the Trace Precedents and Trace Dependents commands to point out such cells.

A *precedent cell* provides data to a specific cell. A *dependent cell* relies on the value of another cell. When you click the Trace Precedents and Trace Dependents buttons on the Formula Auditing toolbar, Excel draws arrows showing precedent and dependent cells.

Do it!

A-1: Tracing precedent and dependent cells

Here's how	Here's why
1 Open Multi user	From the current unit folder.
Save the workbook as **My multi user**	In the current unit folder.
2 Activate the Monthly QOH worksheet	(If necessary.) Monthly QOH worksheet contains a single month's quantity-on-hand totals for seven products.
Observe that the worksheet displays error values in some cells	These error values are indicated by the green triangles that appear in the upper-left corner of the cells.
3 Click F14	An Error Checking smart tag appears.
Click as shown	
Choose **Show Formula Auditing Toolbar**	To display the Formula Auditing toolbar.

4 Select C10	This cell contains the formula =D10/B10.
Click ⊡	```• ——————1.50|► ◄ 3694 ► •5541.00```
	(The Trace Precedents button is on the Formula Auditing toolbar.) To trace the precedent cells of the selected cell. You can see two tracer arrows meeting at C10. These indicate that B10 and D10 provide values for the formula in C10 and are the precedent cells of C10.
5 Click ⊡	(The Remove All Arrows button is on the Formula Auditing toolbar.) To hide all tracer arrows.
6 Click ⊡	

3694	5541.00	4143 ►	449
5265	6581.25	7343	2078
#DIV/0!	6042.40	6782	#DIV/0!
1118	2012.40	3676	2558
			#DIV/0!

	(The Trace Dependents button is on the Formula Auditing toolbar.) To trace the dependent cells of C10. Two tracer arrows point from C10 to F10 and F14. The calculated values of F10 and F14 get their data from C10 and are the dependent cells of C10.
7 Click ⊡	(The Remove All Arrows button is on the Formula Auditing toolbar.) To hide all tracer arrows.
8 Update the workbook	

Tracing errors in a worksheet

Explanation

When Excel detects an error, it displays an error value (in the cell) and an Error Checking smart tag. You can click this smart tag to display a list of commands that can help you trace and correct the error. The Formula Auditing toolbar also provides tools for doing this.

To trace an error, select the cell that contains the error; then, either click the Trace Error button on the Formula Auditing toolbar, or choose the Trace Error command. The Trace Error command is available through the Smart Tag options or the Tools, Formula Auditing submenu.

When you click the Trace Error button, you'll see tracer arrows pointing from the cell containing the error to other cells that provide values for the formula. Red arrows indicate possible sources of the error; blue arrows point to cells that probably are not the cause.

The following table describes the commonly used buttons on the Formula Auditing toolbar:

Button	Name	Description
	Trace Precedents	Draws arrows to the selected cell from any cells that provide values to the formula in it.
	Remove Precedent Arrows	Removes the tracer arrows from precedent cells.
	Trace Dependents	Draws arrows from the selected cell to any cells containing formulas that refer to the selected cell.
	Remove Dependent Arrows	Removes the tracer arrows from dependent cells.
	Remove All Arrows	Removes all tracer arrows from a worksheet.
	Trace Error	Draws tracer arrows connecting the selected cell to all of its precedent and dependent cells. Red tracer arrows point to the cells containing errors. Blue tracer arrows point to dependent cells that do not contain errors.
	New Comment	Inserts a new comment in the worksheet.

Modifying error checking settings

You can modify error checking settings in the Options dialog box. Choose Tools, Options and activate the Error Checking tab. On this tab, you can enable or disable background error checking, and select which error-checking rules you'd like to use.

Do it!   ## A-2:   Tracing errors

Here's how	Here's why
1 Select F14	
Click	
	(The Trace Error button is on the Formula Auditing toolbar.) To display tracer arrows that show the source of the error produced by the formula in F14. A red arrow points to F14 from C12. This arrow indicates that the cause of the error is the invalid value in C12. C12 gets its value from B12 and D12, as indicated by the blue arrows. B12 is empty, which causes the invalid value in C12.
2 In B12, enter **2**	
	To correct the error values. The red arrow disappears, and valid numeric values replace the error values. The blue arrows indicate non-error conditions.
3 Remove the tracer arrows	(Click the Remove All Arrows button on the Formula Auditing toolbar.)
4 Close the Formula Auditing toolbar	
5 Update the workbook	

Topic B: Comments and text boxes

This topic covers the following Microsoft Office Specialist exam objectives.

#	Objective
XL03S-4-1	Adding and editing comments attached to worksheet cells
XL03E-4-6	Managing workbook properties (e.g., summary data)

Viewing comments

Explanation

A *comment* is a note or annotation that you can add to cells to provide additional information. Adding comments to data makes your worksheet convenient for other users to interpret. These comments do not alter the data in the cell. Comments are denoted by small, red triangles, called *comment indicators*, in the upper-right corner of the cells.

To view a comment, point to the cell containing the comment indicator. You can also choose View, Comments to view all the comments in the worksheet simultaneously.

Do it!

B-1: Viewing comments in a worksheet

Here's how	Here's why
1 Observe C9	
	There is a red comment indicator in the upper-right corner of the cell.
2 Point to C9	
	To display the associated comment. By default, cells always display comment indicators but do not display comments until you point to them.
Move the pointer to another cell	The comment disappears.
3 Choose **View**, **Comments**	
	To display all the comments at the same time. The Reviewing toolbar also appears.
4 Click	(The Hide All Comments button is on the Reviewing toolbar.) To hide all the comments.

Adding comments

Comments aid in the interpretation of data. They can also be used to provide additional information about data.

To add a comment, select a cell, choose Insert, Comment, and then enter the text in the comment box that appears. You can also use the New Comment button on the Reviewing toolbar. Used to examine a document, the Reviewing toolbar contains buttons to insert a comment, view a previous comment, view the next comment, or display all comments.

After you've entered a comment, you might want to change or edit it. To do so, click the cell containing the comment you want to edit and choose Insert, Edit Comment. When you're finished making changes, click outside the comment box.

You can also add a comment to a workbook by using the Summary tab of the Properties dialog box, as shown in Exhibit 7-1. This dialog box can also be used to modify other properties of a workbook. On the Summary tab, you can specify workbook details, such as a descriptive title, a subject, an author name, a company name, keywords, and comments.

To add summary information to an open workbook:

1   Choose File, Properties.
2   In the Properties dialog box, on the Summary tab, enter the descriptive information in the appropriate box; for example, enter any comments in the Comments box.
3   Click OK.

You can view workbook properties by selecting the workbook in Windows Explorer. Simply place the mouse pointer over the relevant worksheet icon to view a ScreenTip containing the properties. You can also view properties in Excel in the Open, Save, or Search dialog boxes.

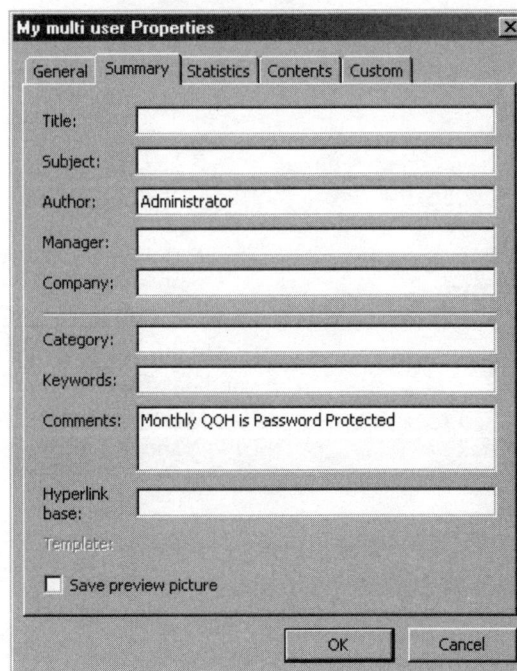

Exhibit 7-1: The Summary tab in the Properties dialog box

Do it!   **B-2:   Adding a comment**

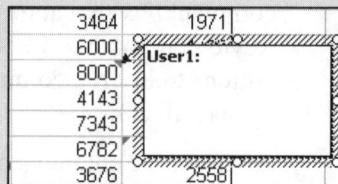

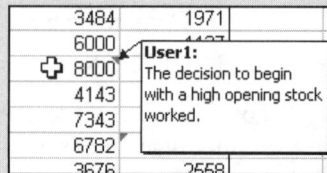

Here's how	Here's why
1 Select E9	
Click ▭	(The New Comment button is on the Reviewing toolbar.) Your user name appears in the comment box. The red comment indicator appears in the upper-right corner of the cell.
Type **The decision to begin with a high opening stock worked.**	To add this information as a comment.
Click outside the comment box	The comment box disappears, but the cell displays the red comment indicator.
2 Point to E9	To view the comment you just added.
3 Choose **File**, **Properties**	To open the Properties dialog box.
In the Title box, type **Monthly Totals**	To create a workbook title.
In the Author box, type your name	To add the name of the workbook author.
In the Comments box, type **Quantity-on-hand**	To enter additional information about the workbook content.
Click **OK**	To add this summary information to the workbook file.
4 Update the workbook	To save these changes.

5 Choose **File**, **Open**	The Open dialog box appears.
Click **My multi user**	To select the workbook file.
Click as shown	
Choose **Properties**	The document properties you created appear on the right side of the Open dialog box.
6 Click **Cancel**	To close the dialog box.
7 Close the Reviewing toolbar	(Choose View, Toolbar, Reviewing to close the Reviewing toolbar.)
8 Update the workbook	

Working with comments

Explanation

By using the View tab in the Options dialog box, you can customize the way comments and comment indicators appear. You can display only indicators, comments and indicators, or nothing at all. The default setting displays only the comment indicators. When you change the comment indicator settings, the new settings will be applied to all new workbooks.

To change comment settings:

1   Choose Tools, Options to open the Options dialog box.
2   Activate the View tab.
3   Under Comments, select the necessary option.
4   Click OK.

Do it!

B-3:   Managing comments

Here's how	Here's why
1 Point to B8	To see the comment associated with the cell.
2 Open the Options dialog box	(Choose Tools, Options.)
Activate the View tab	(If necessary.)
Under Comments, select **None**	
Click **OK**	The comment indicators in the worksheet are no longer visible.
3 Point to B8	You do not see a comment even though there is one attached to the cell.
4 Open the Options dialog box	
Under Comments, select **Comment & indicator**	
Click **OK**	All the comments, and their indicators, appear on the worksheet.
5 Change the Comment setting to **Comment indicator only**	This is the default state.

Creating text boxes

Explanation
You can also add comments or additional information to a worksheet by adding text boxes. Unlike comments, text boxes are always displayed.

To add a text box to a worksheet:

1   Display the Drawing toolbar.
2   On the Drawing toolbar, click the Text Box button. Point to the location where you want to insert the text box.
3   Drag to create the text box.
4   Type the text you want, and then deselect the text box.

Do it!

B-4:   Creating a text box

Here's how	Here's why
1 Display the Drawing toolbar	(If necessary.)
2 Click [A≣]	(The Text Box button is on the Drawing toolbar.) You'll add a text box to the worksheet.
Draw a text box as shown	
	You'll add a heading for the data.
3 In the text box, type **Statement of quantity on hand**	
Click on the text box	To deselect the text and select the text box.
4 Change the font of the text in the text box to **Arial Black**	(Use the Formatting toolbar.)
Specify the size as **12 pt**	(You might have to resize the text box to view the text completely.)
Center the text	
5 Deselect the text box	
6 Update the workbook	

Topic C: Protection

This topic covers the following Microsoft Office Specialist exam objectives.

#	Objective
XL03E-3-1	Adding protection to cells, worksheets and workbooks
XL03E-3-2	Using digital signatures to authenticate workbooks
XL03E-3-2	Setting passwords

Why should I protect my Excel data?

Explanation

By protecting a worksheet, you can prevent unauthorized users from modifying it. You can protect an entire worksheet or protect only a part of it, permitting users to alter the other parts.

Applying password protection to a worksheet

You might need to prevent the data of a worksheet from being altered accidentally or by other users. You can use the Protect Sheet dialog box to password-protect a worksheet. To password-protect a worksheet:

1 Choose Tools, Protection, Protect Sheet to open the Protect Sheet dialog box.
2 Check the options you want.
3 Type a password and click OK. The Confirm Password dialog box will appear.
4 In the Reenter password to proceed box, type the same password. Click OK.

Before entering data into a password-protected sheet, you should unprotect it. To unprotect a sheet, choose Tools, Protection, Unprotect Sheet to open the Unprotect Sheet dialog box. In the Password box, enter the password, and click OK.

Exhibit 7-2: The Protect Sheet dialog box

Protecting a workbook

Similarly, to protect a workbook choose Tools, Protection, Workbook to open the Protect Workbook dialog box. You can protect a workbook's structure and windows. By selecting to protect the structure, you ensure that a workbook can't be moved, deleted, hidden, unhidden, or renamed, and new worksheets can't be inserted. By selecting to protect the windows, you ensure that a workbook's windows are the same size and position each time the workbook is opened. To prevent others from removing workbook protection, you can set a password in this dialog box as well.

Do it!

C-1: Password-protecting a worksheet

Here's how	Here's why
1 Choose **Tools**, **Protection**, **Protect Sheet...**	To open the Protect Sheet dialog box, as shown in Exhibit 7-2. The option Protect worksheet and contents of locked cells is checked by default. In the Allow all users of this worksheet to list, only Select locked cells and Select unlocked cells are checked.
In the Password to unprotect sheet box, type **user1**	
Click **OK**	To open the Confirm Password dialog box.
2 In the Reenter password to proceed box, type **user1**	
Click **OK**	To confirm the password that you entered.
3 Enter a value in B11	A message box appears stating that the cell is protected, and as a result, you cannot enter a value in or change the worksheet.
Click **OK**	
4 Choose **Tools**, **Protection**, **Unprotect Sheet...**	To open the Unprotect Sheet dialog box.
In the Password box, type **user1**	
Click **OK**	
5 In B11, enter **1.5**	You can now enter a value in the worksheet.
6 Update the workbook	

Protecting parts of a worksheet

Explanation

When you password-protect an entire worksheet, all the cells in the worksheet are locked by default. This means that users cannot change any of the cells. To permit users change some specific cells, you must unlock the cells manually before protecting the rest of the worksheet. Users can then change data only in the unlocked cells. The rest of the worksheet remains protected. One typical application of this is to unlock the cells containing raw values to permit data entry, and lock the cells containing formulas.

To protect only a part of a worksheet:

1 Select the range of cells that you want users to be able to modify.
2 Choose Format, Cells to open the Format Cells dialog box. Activate the Protection tab.
3 Clear the Locked check box, and click OK.
4 Protect the worksheet. You don't necessarily need to use a password.

Do it!

C-2:   Protecting part of a worksheet by unlocking cells

Here's how	Here's why
1 Select B7:B13	You'll keep these cells unlocked while protecting the rest of the worksheet.
2 Open the Format Cells dialog box	(Choose Format, Cells.)
Click the **Protection** tab	
Clear **Locked**	
Click **OK**	To unlock the selected range of cells.
3 Open the Protect Sheet dialog box	(Choose Tools, Protection, Protect Sheet.) You'll protect the sheet, but users will be able to modify the unlocked cells in the range B7:B13.
Click **OK**	Because you did not enter a password, any user can unprotect the worksheet by using the Unprotect Sheet dialog box.
4 In B11, enter **2.5**	You can enter the value in the unlocked cell.
5 In D10, enter a value	A message box appears stating that the cell is protected, and as a result, you cannot enter a value in or change the worksheet.
Click **OK**	
6 Update the workbook	

Protecting worksheets by using digital signatures

Explanation

When you send worksheets or other documents through the Internet, there is a chance that someone might access and alter them. To protect your documents from unauthorized access, you can use digital signatures. A *digital signature* is an electronic security stamp that is used to authenticate files that are sent through the Internet. To use a digital signature, you need to install a *digital certificate*, which is an attachment that guarantees security for a file.

To obtain a digital certificate, you should submit an application to a commercial certification authority, such as VeriSign Inc. You can also obtain a digital certificate from your internal security administrator or from an Information Technology professional. It's also possible to create your own digital certificates, called *self-signed projects*. However, self-signed projects might not be legally valid because they are not sanctioned by any legal authority.

When you receive a digital certificate, included are instructions on how to install it on your computer. After installing the certificate, you can use it to sign the files that you send through the Internet.

To use a digital signature:

1   Choose Tools, Options, to open the Options dialog box.
2   Activate the Security tab.
3   Click Digital Signatures to open the Digital Signature dialog box.
4   Select a digital signature from the list.
5   Click OK.

Do it!

C-3:   Discussing digital signatures

Questions and answers
1   What is a digital signature?
2   Why do you need a digital signature?
3   What is a digital certificate?
4   If you create your own digital certificate, is it legally valid?

Topic D: Workgroup collaboration

This topic covers the following Microsoft Office Specialist exam objectives.

#	Objective
XL03E-3-3	Creating and modifying shared workbooks
XL03E-3-4	Merging multiple versions of the same workbook
XL03E-3-5	Track, accept, and reject changes to workbooks
	• Tracking changes
	• Accepting and rejecting changes

Sharing workbooks

Explanation

Sharing a workbook makes it possible for several members of a workgroup to collaborate on the same set of data. For example, several sales managers could enter their respective regional sales figures in the same workbook, eliminating the need to collect and consolidate the data manually.

To share a workbook:

1 Open the workbook that you want to share.

2 Choose Tools, Share Workbook to open the Share Workbook dialog box. Activate the Editing tab.

3 Check Allow changes by more than one user at the same time, and then click OK.

4 Save the workbook in a location where other users can access it.

You can control how a workbook is shared by using the Advanced tab in the Share Workbook dialog box. For example, under Update changes, you can select When file is saved, to see the changes made by other users each time you save the workbook. You can also set the interval at which changes will be shown automatically.

Modifying a shared workbook

To edit a shared workbook, open the workbook from its network location. Create a user name to identify your work by choosing Tools, Options and on the General tab, enter your name in the User name box. Then make changes to the workbook as usual.

When modifying a shared workbook, you won't be able to change the following elements: merged cells, conditional formats, data validation, charts, pictures, objects including drawing objects, hyperlinks, scenarios, outlines, subtotals, data tables, PivotTable reports, workbook and worksheet protection, and macros.

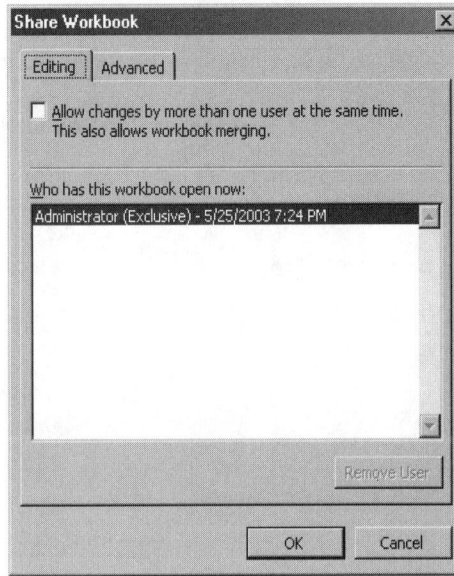

Exhibit 7-3: The Editing tab in the Share Workbook dialog box

Do it!

D-1: Sharing a workbook

Here's how	Here's why
1 Choose **Tools**, **Share Workbook...**	To open the Share Workbook dialog box. By default, the Editing tab is active, as shown in Exhibit 7-3.
2 Check the indicated option as shown	☑ Allow changes by more than one user at the same time. This also allows workbook merging.
Click **OK**	A message box appears, warning you that this action will save the workbook.
Click **OK**	The name of the workbook changes to My multi user [Shared].

Merging workbooks

Explanation

You might need to share a workbook among users who cannot access the same file simultaneously. You can do this by distributing copies of the shared workbook, permitting users to change their copies and then merge those copies into a single workbook.

To share a workbook that you intend to merge later:

1   Open the Share Workbook dialog box, activate the Editing tab, and check Allow changes by more than one user at the same time.

2   On the Advanced tab, under Track changes, select Keep change history for. In the box, enter the number of days you want to permit users to change the workbook. Click OK.

3   Make copies of the workbook, and distribute one to each user.

After the users have changed their copies of the workbook, you can merge the copies into a single workbook. To merge workbooks:

1   Choose Tools, Compare and Merge Workbooks to open the Select Files to Merge Into Current Workbook dialog box.

2   Select the copies of the workbook that contain changes you want to merge.

3   Click OK.

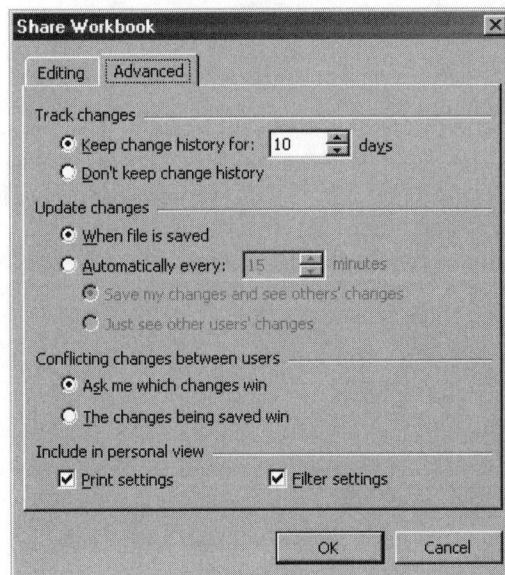

Exhibit 7-4: The Advanced tab in the Share Workbook dialog box

Do it!

D-2:   Merging workbooks

Here's how	Here's why
1 Open the Share Workbook dialog box	(Choose Tools, Share Workbook.)
Click the **Advanced** tab	Under Track changes, Keep change history for is selected. You'll maintain a history of changes made by various users.
Edit the days box to read **10**	(As shown in Exhibit 7-4.) This will permit users to track the change history for 10 days.
Click **OK**	
2 Activate the Sales report worksheet	You'll work on this worksheet.
Update the workbook	
3 Save the workbook as **Copy of my multi user**	You'll merge this workbook with another one.
4 Select A4:E4	
Apply Pale Blue shading to the selection	(Use the arrow on the Fill Color button on the Formatting toolbar.) You'll change the format of the data, and see the changes being applied to the workbook My multi user.
5 Apply Aqua shading to A5:A14	
6 Apply Pale Blue shading to A15:E15	
Deselect the range	
Update and close the workbook	
7 Open My multi user	
Save the workbook as **Copy2 of my multi user**	You'll consolidate the changes by merging the two copies of the workbook with the original workbook.
8 Verify that Sales report is the active worksheet	
In B5, enter **840**	
Update and close the workbook	

9 Open My multi user

10 Choose **Tools**, **Compare and Merge Workbooks...**

(To open the Select Files to Merge Into Current Workbook dialog box.) You'll update the current workbook with the changes you made in Copy of my multi user and Copy2 of my multi user.

Select **Copy of my multi user**

Press (CTRL) and select **Copy2 of my multi user**

Click **OK**

11 Activate the Sales report sheet

(If necessary.) The format of the data changes to what you had applied in Copy of my multi user. The ranges A4:E4 and A15:E15 now have Pale Blue shading. The range A5:E14 has Aqua shading. Also, the value in B5 changes to $840.00, the value you specified in Copy2 of my multi user.

12 Update the workbook

Tracking changes

Explanation

You can examine the changes made in a workbook by using the Track Changes feature. This helps you identify who made the changes, when they were made, what the original values were, and what the new values are. If your workbook is not shared, Excel makes the workbook shared automatically when you turn on the Track Changes feature.

To highlight changes:

1 Choose Tools, Track Changes, Highlight Changes to open the Highlight Changes dialog box.

2 If the workbook is not shared, check Track changes while editing. If the workbook is shared, this option will be checked by default.

3 Specify how you want the changes to be tracked:

- If you want to view changes based on when they were made—for example, after a specific date—check When, and then select the necessary setting from the list.

- If you want to view the changes made by a specific user, check Who, and then select Everyone or Everyone but Me from the list.

- If you want to view the changes made to a specific range of cells, check Where, and then enter the range.

4 Click OK.

To review workbook changes and accept or reject them:

1 Open the workbook that contains the tracked changes.

2 Choose Tools, Track Changes, Accept or Reject Changes. You'll be prompted to save the workbook.

3 Click OK to save the workbook. The Select Changes to Accept or Reject dialog box appears.

4 If you want to view changes based on when they were made, check When and then select a time setting.

5 Click OK to open the Accept or Reject Changes dialog box. At the same time, a cell that contains a changed value will be highlighted. This dialog box displays information about each change, including the name of the person who made the change, the date and time it was made, and other changes that will occur if you accept or reject the suggested change. You can scroll down to view the rest of the contents.

6 Click Accept to accept the change, or click Reject to restore the original value. The next cell with a changed value will be highlighted.

Do it!

D-3:   Tracking changes in a workbook

Here's how	Here's why
1 Activate the Profit projection sheet	
2 In B7, enter **60000**	This is the new total sales value for Qtr 1.
3 Choose **Tools**, **Track Changes**, **Highlight Changes...**	To open the Highlight Changes dialog box. By default, Since I last saved is entered in the When box, and Everyone is entered in the Who box.
Click **OK**	
4 Point to B7	A comment appears, stating that the value in B7 has changed from $50,000.00 to $60,000.00.
5 Choose **Tools**, **Track Changes**, **Accept or Reject Changes...**	A message box appears, stating that the workbook will be saved.
Click **OK**	
	To open the Select Changes to Accept or Reject dialog box. By default, the When box is checked.
Click **OK**	To open the Accept or Reject Changes dialog box, which shows that B5 was changed.
6 Click **Accept**	The dialog box shows that B7 was changed.
7 Click **Reject**	The original value in B7 is restored.
8 Update and close the workbook	

Unit summary: Documenting and auditing

Topic A
In this topic, you learned how to use the **Formula Auditing** toolbar to **trace precedent** and **dependent** cells and to view the relationships between formulas in a worksheet. You learned that a precedent cell provides a value to another cell, and a dependent cell depends on another cell for a value. You also learned how to **trace errors**.

Topic B
In this topic, you learned how to **add comments** to cells. You learned that a comment is used to provide additional information about data. You also learned how to **display one comment at a time** and how to **display all comments** together. In addition, you learned how to **change** the **comment indicator** settings. You also learned how to add **text boxes** to display text information.

Topic C
In this topic, you learned how to **password-protect** a worksheet to prevent unauthorized users from changing it. You also learned how to protect only a part of a worksheet by **unlocking cells** that you want users to be able to modify. You also learned about **digital signatures**.

Topic D
In this topic, you learned how to **share workbooks** and how to **merge copies** of shared workbooks that various users have changed. You learned that sharing a workbook permits multiple users to work on it at the same time. You also learned how to **track changes** in a workbook and how to **accept** or **reject** tracked changes.

Independent practice activity

1 Open Practice multi user, and save it as **My practice multi user**.

2 In B7, add this comment: **The constantly increasing fixed cost prevented the profit percentage from increasing.**

3 In the range A1:F2, add a text box with the text **Statement of profit**. Format the text as 14 pt., Times New Roman, and center it. Resize the text box if necessary.

4 Trace the cells causing the error value in F10.

5 Trace the precedent and dependent cells of D6.

6 Compare your result with Exhibit 7-5.

7 Remove all arrows, and close the Formula Auditing toolbar.

8 Close the Reviewing toolbar. (If necessary.)

9 Unlock B4:C13; then protect the worksheet with a password.

10 Update the workbook.

11 Share the workbook, allowing changes by more than one user at a time.

12 Save the workbook as **Copy of my practice multi user**. Then, in the Sales analysis sheet, apply Plum shading to A6:E6, and Gray 25% shading to A8:E22. When you're done, update the workbook and close it.

13 Open My practice multi user.

14 Merge My practice multi user with Copy of my practice multi user, and observe the changes in the Sales analysis sheet.

15 In the Sales report sheet, in A3, enter **Name**. In E5, enter **5000**. Track the changes you made. Restore the original value in A3. Accept the change in E5.

16 Update and close the workbook.

	A	B	C	D	E	F
1						
2			Statement of profit			
3	Year	Fixed cost	Variable cost	Total cost	Total revenue	%Profit
4	1996	60000	55000	115000	135000	15%
5	1997	80000	75000	155000	160000	3%
6	1998	90000	80000	170000	182000	7%
7	1999	96000	86000	182000	195000	7%
8	2000	102000	85000	187000	207000	10%
9	2001	107000	85000	192000	222000	14%
10	2002	107500	88000	195500		#DIV/0!
11	2003	109000	90000	199000	225000	12%
12	2004	110000	96000	206000	236000	13%
13	2005	110000	98000	208000	240000	13%

Exhibit 7-5: The worksheet after Step 5

Review questions

1 What are precedent and dependent cells? How can you identify them in a worksheet?

2 When you click the Trace Error button, you'll see red and blue tracer arrows pointing from the cell containing the error to other cells. What do the red and blue arrows mean?

3 List the steps you would use to password protect a worksheet.

4 If you choose to protect a workbook's structure, what kinds of changes are affected?

5 What is a digital signature?

Unit 8

Using templates

Unit time: 35 minutes

Complete this unit, and you'll know how to:

A Use Excel's built-in templates to create invoices and expense reports.

B Create and manage custom templates.

Topic A: Built-in templates

This topic covers the following Microsoft Office Specialist exam objective.

#	Objective
XL03S-5-1	Creating a workbook from a template

What is a template?

Explanation

You can use a template to create multiple workbooks that have the same settings, such as formatting and style. A *template* is a workbook with predefined settings on which you can base new workbooks. Templates can contain labels and other data, formatting, styles, and functionality such as formulas.

The Templates dialog box

Excel provides several built-in templates that help you create forms, such as invoices, purchase orders, and expense statements. You can view Excel's built-in templates by activating the Spreadsheet Solutions tab in the Templates dialog box, as shown in Exhibit 8-1.

[handwritten note in left margin: Open new sheet — View / Taskpane]

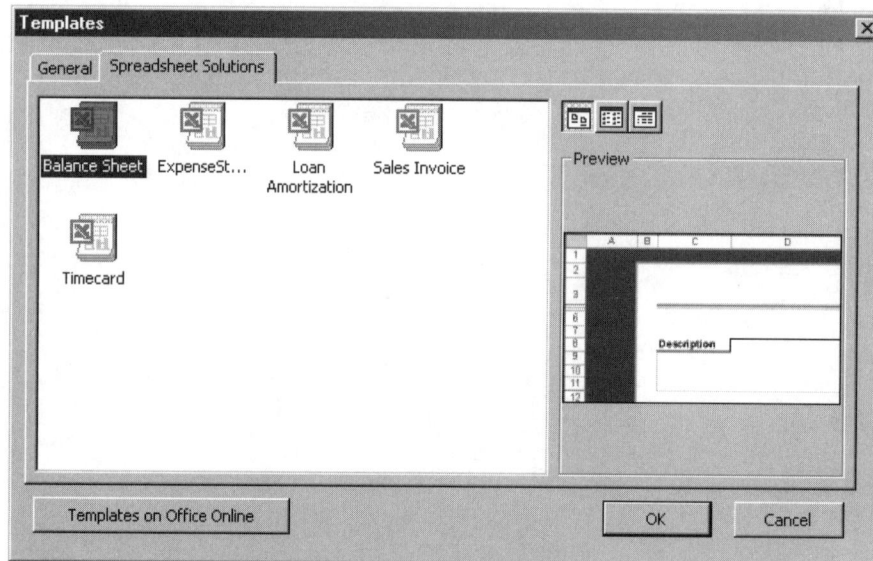

Exhibit 8-1: The Spreadsheet Solutions tab in the Templates dialog box

Creating a workbook from a template

You can use the Sales Invoice template to create invoices you send to customers. In a sales invoice, you can include company details (such as name and address), customer details, order details, and payment details. To use the Sales Invoice template:

1 Choose File, New to open the New Workbook task pane.

2 Under Other templates, click On my computer to open the Templates dialog box.

3 Activate the Spreadsheet Solutions tab.

4 Double-click Sales Invoice.

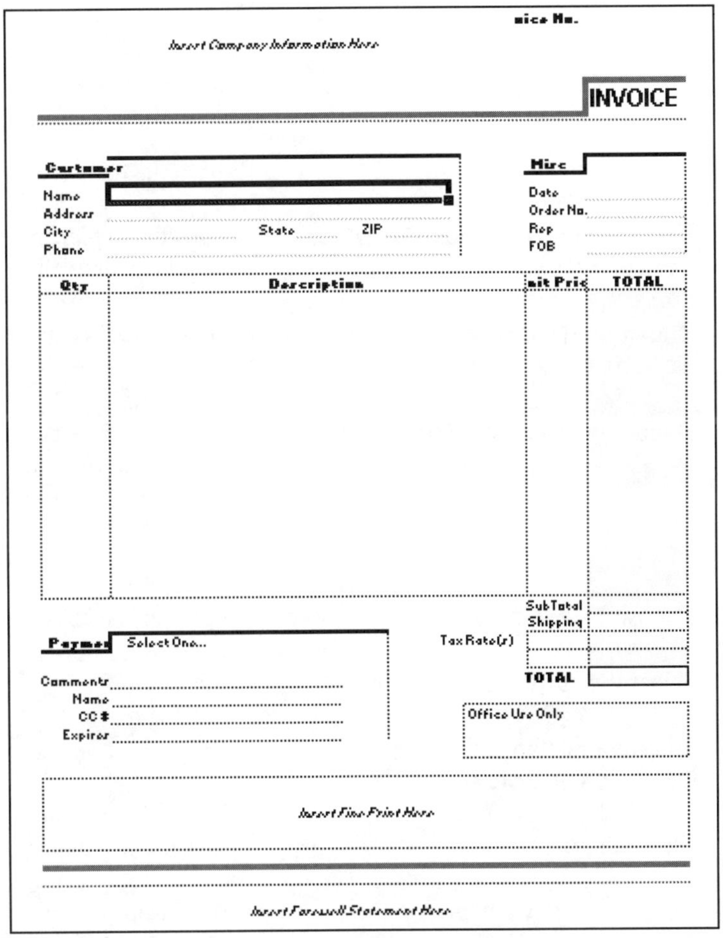

Exhibit 8-2: The Sales Invoice template form

A-1: Using the Sales Invoice template

Here's how	Here's why
1 Choose **File**, **New…**	

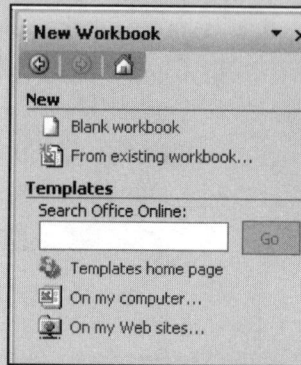

> **New Workbook** ▾ ✕
>
> ⊕ ⊖ ⌂
>
> **New**
> 📄 Blank workbook
> 📄 From existing workbook…
>
> **Templates**
> Search Office Online:
> [   ] [Go]
>
> 📄 Templates home page
> 📄 On my computer…
> 📄 On my Web sites…

	To open the New Workbook task pane.
Under Templates, click **On my computer…**	To open the Templates dialog box. It has two tabs: General and Spreadsheet Solutions.
Click the **Spreadsheet Solutions** tab	A group of icons appears, representing Excel's built-in templates.
Double-click **Sales Invoice**	The title bar of the new workbook displays Sales Invoice1, indicating that this is a form based on the Sales Invoice template. The form is not filled out but includes text, formulas, and several placeholders, as shown in Exhibit 8-2.
2 Choose **File**, **Save As…**	To open the Save As dialog box.
Select the current unit folder	
Edit the File name box to read **OS sales invoice**	
Click **Save**	To save the workbook as OS sales invoice.
3 Click **Insert Company Information Here**	(A ScreenTip appears providing information on how to enter multiple lines in a single cell.) You'll add the company details in this cell.
Enter the indicated Company details	

> *Company name*
> *Company address*
> *City*
> *State*

You can use Alt+Enter to enter multiple lines in a single cell.

4 Enter the indicated Customer details

Customer	
Name	Adam Hayward
Address	Ulster Street
City	Denver State CO ZIP 80237
Phone	(720) 528-1700

5 Enter the indicated Qty, Description, and Unit Price details

Qty	Description	Unit Price	TOTAL
25	Cassia	$ 750.00	$ 18,750.00
45	Cilanto Flakes	$ 800.00	$ 36,000.00

The TOTAL value for each product is calculated automatically when you enter the Qty and Unit Price. The SubTotal and TOTAL values for the entire invoice are also calculated automatically.

6 Next to Payment, click **Select One**

A drop-down arrow appears and a ScreenTip prompts you to select a payment type.

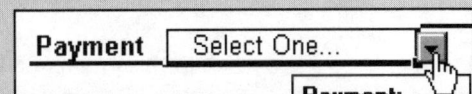

Click as shown

Payment	Select One... ▼
	Payment:

To display a list of payment options.

Select **Credit**

7 Enter the remaining payment details as indicated

Payment	Credit
Comments	
Name	Adam Hayward
CC #	3767879
Expires	Feb-05

Enter the expiration date as 02/28/05.

8 Observe the Insert Fine Print Here cell

This cell can be used for disclaimers, warranty information, and similar text.

9 Click **Insert Farewell Statement Here**

This cell is intended for thank-you messages, company slogans, and other notes. You'll add a slogan.

Press (DELETE)

To delete the contents of the cell.

Type **Quality and reliability in products**

10 Update and close the workbook

The ExpenseStatement template

Explanation

You can use the ExpenseStatement template to create workbooks that track expenses for a specific pay period. You can include employee details, such as name, SSN, and department, as well as details about your expenses for a specific period.

To use the ExpenseStatement template, open in the Templates dialog box. On the Spreadsheet Solutions tab, choose ExpenseStatement.

Do it!

A-2: Using the ExpenseStatement template

Here's how	Here's why
1 Open the New Workbook task pane	(Choose File, New.)
Open the Templates dialog box	(Click On my computer.)
Double-click **ExpenseStatement**	The title bar of the new workbook displays ExpenseStatement1, indicating that this is a form based on the ExpenseStatement template.
2 Open the Save As dialog box	
Edit the File name box to read **OS expense statement**	(From the Save in list, select the current unit folder, if necessary.)
Click **Save**	

3 Under Employee, enter the indicated employee details

Employee			
Name	Allan Calvin	Emp #	23
SSN	142-22-3465	Position	Marketing Manager
Department	Marketing	Manager	Jim Calahan

4 Under Pay Period, enter the indicated data

Pay Period	
From	3/1/2005
To	3/31/2005

5 Enter the indicated expense details for Allan Calvin

Date	Account	Description	Lodging	Transport	Fuel	Meals	Phone	Entertainment
3/10/2005	2235	Site Visit	$ 180.00	$ 45.00	$ 5.00	$ 15.00	$ 4.00	
3/23/2005	2235	Client Visit	$ 150.00	$ 40.00	$ 5.00	$ 15.00	$ 6.00	

6 Update and close the workbook

Topic B: Creating and managing templates

This topic covers the following Microsoft Office Specialist exam objectives.

#	Objective
XL03E-4-4	Create and edit templates
	• Creating a workbook template
	• Creating a new workbook based upon a user-defined template
	• Editing a workbook template
XL03E-5-3	Changing the default file location for templates

Creating and using templates

Explanation

If the built-in templates in Excel do not contain all the functionality you need, you can create your own custom templates. As with built-in templates, you can use custom templates to create and maintain multiple workbooks with the same formatting, styles, content, and functionality.

To create a template:

1   Open or create the workbook on which you want to base the template.
2   Choose File, Save As to open the Save As dialog box.
3   From the Save as type list, select Template.
4   In the File name box, enter a name for the template.
5   Click Save.

Do it!

B-1:   Creating a template

Here's how	Here's why
1 Open Sample test	(From the current unit folder.) You'll use this workbook as the basis for a new template. The Sample test workbook contains two linked worksheets: Observations and Results.
2 Open the Save As dialog box	
From the Save as type list, select **Template**	To create a template file based on this workbook. The Save in box shows Templates, indicating that Excel saves templates in the Templates folder by default. The File name box shows Sample test, indicating that Excel saves the template with the name of the workbook on which it's based.
Click **Save**	To create the Sample test template.
3 Close the template	

4   Choose **File**, **New**   To open the New Workbook task pane. You'll create a new workbook based on the Sample test template.

Under Templates, click **On my Computer...**   To open the Templates dialog box.

Click the **General** tab

Select **Sample test**

Click **OK**

5   Save the workbook as **S001 test**   In the current unit folder.

6   Under Sample Details, enter the indicated information

Product	Anise Seed
Sample Code	S001
Test Type	T005
Sample Date	12/2/2005

7   Under Test Details, enter the indicated information

Test No.	Test Date& Time	Observations
1	20/12/2005 11:30 a.m.	Initial Color-White, Final Color-Yellow
2	20/12/2005 12:30 p.m.	Initial Color-Yellow, Final Color-Brown

8   Activate the Results sheet   The data under Sample Details from the Observations worksheet has been inserted automatically in the Results worksheet.

9   Update and close the workbook

Modifying templates

Explanation

You might sometimes need to modify custom templates. To do so:

1 Choose File, Open.
2 Specify the location and the name of the template file.
3 Click Open.
4 Make the changes, and update the template.

Do it!

B-2: Modifying a template

Here's how	Here's why
1 Open the Sample test template	(Use the File, Open command.) The template is stored in the Templates folder. On a Windows 2000 computer with an installation of Excel with default settings, the folder will be C:\Documents and Settings\User_name\Application Data\Microsoft\Templates.
2 In A11, enter **Tested By**	
3 Apply the formatting of A10 to A11	(Use the Format Painter button.)
4 Copy the contents of A11	
Activate the Results sheet	
Paste the contents in A11	
5 Activate the Observations sheet	To ensure that this is the active worksheet when the template is saved.
6 Update and close the template	
7 Create a new workbook based on the Sample test template	(The template is in the General tab of the Templates dialog box.) You can see the changes you made to the template.
8 Close the workbook	You need not save changes.

Using an alternate template location

Explanation

When you save a workbook as a template on a Windows 2000 computer, by default the template is saved in the C:\Documents and Settings\User_name\Application Data\Microsoft\Templates folder. If you have a template stored in a location other than this default folder, it will not automatically appear in the New Workbook task pane.

To specify an alternate template location and have Excel open those templates automatically:

1 Choose Tools, Options to open the Options dialog box.

2 Click the General tab.

3 In the At startup, open all files in box, type the path where the template files are located.

4 Click OK.

5 Close Excel.

6 Start Excel. Your templates will now be available in the New Workbook task pane. In the task pane, click On my computer to open the Templates dialog box, and view your templates on the General tab.

Note: Any files stored in this alternate file location will be opened automatically by Excel upon startup. Be sure that this location contains only files that Excel can read, such as .xls and .xlt files.

Do it!

B-3: Using an alternate template location

Here's how	Here's why
1 Choose **File**, **Open...**	The Open dialog box appears.
Double-click **Alternate Template**	To open the folder, which contains an alternate sample test template, called Alt Template.
Click **Cancel**	To close the dialog box without opening any files.
2 Choose **File**, **New...**	
Click **On my computer...**	Because the alternate sample test template is not located in the default template folder, it's not readily available in the Templates dialog box.
Click **Cancel**	To close the Templates dialog box.
3 Choose **Tools, Options...**	The Options dialog box appears.
Click the **General** tab	To display General options.
In the At startup, open all files in box, type **C:\Student Data\Unit_08\Alternate Template**	To specify the alternate template file location.
Click **OK**	

4 Close Excel

5 Start Excel

6 Choose **File**, **New...**   The New Workbook task pane appears.

   Click **On my computer...**   The Templates dialog box appears with Alt Template now available.

7 Click **Cancel**   To close the Templates dialog box. You can change or delete the alternate template file location by changing or deleting the contents of the At startup, open all files in box.

8 Choose **Tools, Options...**   The Options dialog box appears.

   Click the **General** tab   To display General options.

   In the At startup, open all files in box, select the path

   Press **Delete**   To delete the path.

   Click **OK**   The alternate template file location is removed.

Unit summary: Using templates

Topic A   In this topic, you learned about **templates**. You learned that templates can be used as a base to create multiple workbooks. You also learned how to use the built-in **Sales Invoice** and **ExpenseStatement** templates to **create** and **maintain invoices** and **expense statements**.

Topic B   In this topic, you learned how to **create custom templates** that contain your preferred formatting, styles, content, and functionality. You also learned how to **modify a custom template** and **specify an alternate template file location**.

Independent practice activity

1 Create a new workbook based on the built-in Sales Invoice template, and save the workbook as **Spice house invoice** in the current unit folder.

2 Customize the form to include company details as shown in Exhibit 8-3.

3 Save the workbook as a template named **OS invoice**.

4 Close the template.

5 Create a new workbook based on the OS invoice template.

6 Enter the customer details in the OS invoice1 form, as shown in Exhibit 8-4.

7 Update and close the workbook.

8 Close Excel.

```
Outlander Spices
61 Rock Creek Dr
Portland Or 97201
Ph: 555-735-0948
```

Exhibit 8-3: The company details for Step 2

				INVOICE

Customer

				Misc	
Name	The Spice House			Date	2/10/2005
Address	411 Princeton Avenue			Order No.	1245
City	Astoria	State OR	ZIP 87103	Rep	
Phone	(526) 563-2440			FOB	

Qty	Description	Unit Price	TOTAL
20	Cinnamon	$ 650.00	$ 13,000.00
15	Nutmeg	$ 300.00	$ 4,500.00
25	Bay Leaf	$ 400.00	$ 10,000.00

Exhibit 8-4: The customer details for Step 6

Review questions

1   What worksheet elements can be contained in a template?

2   Where can you view Excel's built-in templates?

3   List the steps you would use to modify a custom template.

4   When you save a workbook as a template on a Windows 2000 computer, in what folder is it saved by default?

5   If a template is stored in a location other than the default folder, it will not automatically appear in the New Workbook task pane. True or False?

Appendix A
Web discussions

This appendix covers this additional topic:

A Web discussions.

Topic A: Creating and responding to Web discussions

Explanation

You can use Excel's Web Discussions feature to attach comments to Web pages or files that you can open in a browser, such as .xls, .ppt, or .doc files. The comments you attach will appear with the documents but will be stored separately on a discussion server.

Discussion server

To use the Web Discussions feature, you need to connect to a discussion server. A *discussion server* is a computer that stores information such as the location of the document being discussed and its comments.

Here is how you select a discussion server:

1 Choose Tools, Online Collaboration, Web Discussions to display the Web Discussions toolbar.

2 Click Discussions; then choose Discussion Options to open the Discussion Options dialog box. You can also open the Discussion Options dialog box by clicking the Insert Discussion about the Workbook button on the Web Discussions toolbar and clicking Yes.

3 Under Select a discussion server, click Add to open the Add or Edit Discussion Servers dialog box.

4 Enter the name of a discussion server.

5 Click OK to close the Add or Edit Discussion Servers dialog box. Click OK to close the Discussion Options dialog box.

All discussions are *threaded*. This means that the replies or comments appear below the related comment and not in an alphabetical or chronological order.

Adding discussion comments

To add a specific comment to text, first place the insertion point within the text. Then, on the Web Discussions toolbar, click the Insert Discussion in the Document button.

You can also add general comments about a document. To do so, click the Insert Discussions about the Document button. Enter the discussion subject and discussion text, and click OK. The discussion comments will appear in the Discussion pane.

Discussion permissions

To participate in Web discussions, your system administrator must assign you permissions. These permissions will determine the extent to which you can participate in discussions. There are four discussion permissions:

- View Web Document Discussions — You can only view the discussions in a document.

- Author Web Document Discussions — You can reply to comments, insert new comments, or edit and delete your comments.

- Close Web Document Discussions — You can do all of the above and close discussions.

- Manage Web Document Discussions — With this, in addition to Author Discussions permission, you can delete discussions from the Web server.

Filtering discussions

You can also filter the comments entered by a specific reviewer or the comments entered during a specific time frame. To do this:

1   On the Web Discussions toolbar, click Discussions. Choose Filter Discussions.

2   In the Created by box, enter the name of the reviewer whose comments you want to view.

3   In the Creation time box, specify a time frame during which the comments were inserted.

Responding to comments

To reply to a comment, click Show a menu of actions at the end of the discussion comment, and click Reply. You can also edit or delete discussion comments that you have entered.

Do it!

A-1:   Creating and responding to discussion comments

Questions and answers

1   When would you use the Web Discussions feature of Excel?

2   What is a discussion server?

3   What is meant by threaded discussions?

4   List the four discussion permissions

5   How do you add general comments about the document?

6   How do you add a comment to specific text?

Appendix B

Microsoft Office Specialist exam objectives maps

This appendix covers these additional topics:

A Excel 2003 Specialist exam objectives with references to corresponding material in Course ILT courseware.

B Excel 2003 Expert exam objectives with references to corresponding material in Course ILT courseware.

Topic A: Specialist exam objectives

Explanation   The following table lists all Excel 2003 Specialist exam objectives and provides references to the conceptual material and activities that teach each objective.

Objective	Course level	Conceptual information	Supporting activities
Entering, editing, and clearing text, numbers and symbols in cells	Basic	Unit 2, Topic B, pp 4, 6 Unit 2, Topic C, pp 10-11	B-1, B-2 C-1
Fill series content using the fill handle tool	Basic	Unit 3, Topic B, p 14	B-3
Finding and modifying or replacing cell content or formatting	Basic	Unit 2, Topic B, p 8 Unit 5, Topic D, p 24	B-3 D-3
Navigate to specific content (e.g., Go To)	Basic	Unit 1, Topic D, p 16	D-2
Locating supporting information in local reference materials or on the Internet using the Research tool	Basic	Unit 1, Topic C, pp 8, 10-11 Unit 6, Topic A, p 4	C-1, C-2, C-3 A-2
Using the Research tool to select and insert supporting text-based information	Basic	Unit 6, Topic A, p 4	A-2
Inserting, positioning, and sizing graphics	Intermediate	Unit 6, Topic C, pp 10, 14	C-1, C-3
Filtering lists using AutoFilter	Intermediate	Unit 5, Topic B, p 6	B-3
Sorting lists	Intermediate	Unit 5, Topic B, pp 3-4	B-1, B-2
Creating and editing formulas	Basic	Unit 2, Topic C, pp 10-13	C-1, C-2, C-3
Entering a range within a formula by dragging	Basic	Unit 4, Topic A, p 5	A-2
Using references (absolute and relative)	Basic	Unit 3, Topic B, p 12 Unit 3, Topic C, pp 15, 17	B-2 C-1, C-2
Creating formulas using the following function categories: Statistical, Date and Time, Financial, and Logical (e.g., Sum, Min, Max, Date or Now, PMT, IF, Average)	Basic Intermediate Advanced	Unit 4, Topic A, pp 2-3, 5-6 Unit 4, Topic C, pp 10, 12-13 Unit 4, Topic C, pp 16, 18 Unit 1, Topic B, p 10 Unit 1, Topic D, p 18	A-1, A-2, A-3 C-1, C-2, C-3 C-2, C-3 B-1 D-1
Creating, modifying, and positioning diagrams and charts based on data contained in the active workbook	Basic Intermediate	Unit 7, Topic A, pp 2, 6 Unit 7, Topic B, pp 8, 12 Unit 6, Topic C, p 14	A-1, A-3 B-1, B-3 C-3
Formatting cells	Basic	Unit 5, Topic A, p 5	A-3

Objective	Course level	Conceptual information	Supporting activities
Applying AutoFormats to cells and cell ranges	Basic	Unit 5, Topic D, p 22	D-2
Applying styles (e.g., applying a style from the Format>Style list)	Intermediate	Unit 4, Topic D, pp 19, 21	D-2
Modifying height and width	Basic	Unit 5, Topic B, p 7	B-1
Inserting and deleting, hiding and unhiding rows and columns	Basic	Unit 3, Topic D, pp 20-21	D-2, D-3
	Intermediate	Unit 1, Topic B, p 6	B-1
Modifying alignment	Basic	Unit 5, Topic B, p 9	B-2
Formatting tab color, sheet name, and background	Intermediate	Unit 2, Topic A, p 4 Unit 4, Topic A, p 4	A-2 A-2
Hiding and unhiding worksheets	Intermediate	Unit 1, Topic B, p 6	B-1
Adding and editing comments attached to worksheet cells	Intermediate	Unit 7, Topic B, p 7	B-2
Creating a workbook from a template	Intermediate	Unit 8, Topic A, pp 2-3, 6	A-1, A-2
Inserting and deleting selected cells	Basic	Unit 3, Topic D, pp 18, 21	D-1, D-3
Cutting, copying and pasting/pasting special selected cells	Basic	Unit 3, Topic A, pp 2, 4 Unit 5, Topic B, p 7	A-1, A-2
Moving selected cells	Basic	Unit 3, Topic A, pp 2, 6	A-1, A-3
Inserting and editing hyperlinks	Basic	Unit 8, Topic B, p 6	B-1
Inserting worksheets into a workbook	Intermediate	Unit 2, Topic A, p 6	A-3
Deleting worksheets from a workbook	Intermediate	Unit 2, Topic A, p 6	A-3
Repositioning worksheets in a workbook	Intermediate	Unit 2, Topic A, p 6	A-3
Previewing print and Web pages	Basic	Unit 6, Topic A, p 5 Unit 8, Topic A, p 2	A-3 A-1
Previewing page breaks	Intermediate	Unit 1, Topic C, p 14	C-3
Splitting and arranging workbooks	Intermediate	Unit 2, Topic E, p 21	E-1
Splitting, freezing/unfreezing, arranging and hiding/unhiding workbooks	Intermediate	Unit 1, Topic A, pp 4-5 Unit 2, Topic E, p 21	A-2, A-3
Setting print areas	Basic	Unit 6, Topic C, p 17	C-2
Modifying worksheet orientation	Basic	Unit 6, Topic B, p 7	B-1
Adding headers and footers to worksheets	Basic	Unit 6, Topic B, p 11	B-3
Viewing and modifying page breaks	Intermediate	Unit 1, Topic C, pp 13-14	C-2, C-3

Objective	Course level	Conceptual information	Supporting activities
Setting Page Setup options for printing (e.g.; margins, print area, rows/columns to repeat)	Basic	Unit 6, Topic B, pp 9, 13	B-2, B-4
Printing selections, worksheets, and workbooks	Basic	Unit 6, Topic C, pp 15, 17	C-1, C-2
Creating and using folders for workbook storage	Basic	Unit 2, Topic D, pp 14-15	D-1
Renaming folders	Basic	Unit 2, Topic D, pp 14	
Converting files to different file formats for transportability (e.g., .csv, .txt)	Advanced	Unit 5, Topic A, p 2	A-1
Saving selections, worksheets or workbooks as Web pages	Basic	Unit 8, Topic A, pp 2, 4	A-1, A-2

Topic B: Expert exam objectives

Explanation   The following table lists all Excel 2003 Expert exam objectives and provides references to the conceptual material and activities that teach each objective.

Objective	Course level	Conceptual information	Supporting activities
Adding subtotals to worksheet data	Advanced	Unit 3, Topic A, p 2	A-1
Creating and applying advanced filters	Intermediate	Unit 5, Topic C, pp 7-9	C-1, C-2
Grouping and outlining data	Intermediate	Unit 1, Topic B, pp 8-9	B-2
Adding data validation criteria to cells	Advanced	Unit 3, Topic B, pp 5, 7	B-1, B-2
Creating and modifying list ranges	Intermediate	Unit 5, Topic C, p 12	C-3
Managing scenarios	Advanced	Unit 6, Topic C, pp 11, 14-15	C-1, C-2, C-3
Projecting values using analysis tools (e.g., Analysis ToolPak)	Advanced	Unit 6, Topic B, pp 7-8, 10	B-2
Performing What-If analysis	Advanced	Unit 6, Topic A, pp 2, 4	A-1, A-2
Using the Solver add-in	Advanced	Unit 6, Topic A, p 4	A-2
Creating PivotTable Reports and PivotChart Reports	Advanced	Unit 4, Topic A, pp 2-3 Unit 4, Topic D, p 14	A-1 D-1
Using Lookup and Reference functions (e.g., HLOOKUP, VLOOKUP)	Advanced	Unit 2, Topic A, pp 2, 4-5 Unit 2, Topic B, pp 6, 8	A-1, A-2, A-3 B-1, B-2
Creating and editing Database functions (e.g., DSUM, DAVERAGE)	Advanced	Unit 3, Topic C, pp 10-11, 13	C-1, C-2
Tracing formula precedents	Intermediate	Unit 7, Topic A, p 2	A-1
Tracing formula dependents	Intermediate	Unit 7, Topic A, p 2	A-1
Tracing formula errors	Intermediate	Unit 7, Topic A, p 4	A-2
Using Error Checking	Intermediate	Unit 7, Topic A, p 4	A-2
Circling invalid data	Advanced	Unit 3, Topic B, p 5	
Using Evaluate formulas	Advanced	Unit 1, Topic C, p 15	C-2
Using cell Watch	Intermediate	Unit 2, Topic B, p 11	B-2
Naming one or more cell ranges	Advanced	Unit 1, Topic A, pp 2, 6, 8	A-1, A-2, A-3
Using a named range reference in a formula	Advanced	Unit 1, Topic A, p 8	A-3

Objective	Course level	Conceptual information	Supporting activities
Adding, modifying and deleting maps	Advanced	Unit 5, Topic B, pp 6-7, 12	B-1, B-4
Managing elements and attributes in XML workbooks (e.g., adding, modifying, deleting, cutting, copying)	Advanced	Unit 5, Topic B, pp 6-7, 10	B-1, B-3
Defining XML options (e.g., applying XML view options)	Advanced	Unit 5, Topic B, pp 6-7	B-1
Creating and applying custom number formats	Intermediate	Unit 4, Topic B, p 10	B-3
Using conditional formatting	Basic	Unit 5, Topic C, p 18	C-3
Using cropping and rotating tools	Intermediate	Unit 6, Topic C, p 14	C-3
Controlling image contrast and brightness	Intermediate	Unit 6, Topic C, p 14	C-3
Scaling and resizing graphics	Intermediate	Unit 6, Topic C, p 14	C-3
Applying formats to charts and diagrams (e.g., data series, plot area)	Basic	Unit 7, Topic B, p 10	B-2
Adding protection to cells, worksheets and workbooks	Intermediate	Unit 7, Topic C, pp 12-14	C-1, C-2
Using digital signatures to authenticate workbooks	Intermediate	Unit 7, Topic C, p 15	C-3
Setting passwords	Intermediate	Unit 7, Topic C, p 13	C-1
Setting macro settings	Advanced	Unit 7, Topic A, pp 2, 6	A-3
Creating and modifying shared workbooks	Intermediate	Unit 7, Topic D, pp 16-17	D-1
Merging multiple versions of the same workbook	Intermediate	Unit 7, Topic D, p 19	D-2
Tracking changes	Intermediate	Unit 7, Topic D, p 22	D-3
Accepting and rejecting changes	Intermediate	Unit 7, Topic D, p 22	D-3
Bringing information into Excel from external sources	Advanced	Unit 5, Topic C, p 13	C-1
Linking to Web page data	Advanced	Unit 5, Topic C, pp 16-17	C-3
Exporting structured data from Excel	Advanced	Unit 5, Topic B, p 10	B-3
Publishing Web-based worksheets	Basic	Unit 8, Topic A, p 4	A-2
Creating a workbook template	Intermediate	Unit 8, Topic B, p 7	B-1
Creating a new workbook based upon a user-defined template	Intermediate	Unit 8, Topic B, p 7	B-1

Objective	Course level	Conceptual information	Supporting activities
Editing a workbook template	Intermediate	Unit 8, Topic B, p 9	B-2
Consolidating data from two or more worksheets	Intermediate	Unit 2, Topic C, pp 12-13	C-1
Managing workbook properties (e.g., summary data)	Intermediate	Unit 7, Topic B, p 7	B-2
Adding and removing buttons from toolbars	Intermediate	Unit 3, Topic B, p 15	B-3
Adding custom menus	Intermediate	Unit 3, Topic B, p 18	B-4
Creating macros	Advanced	Unit 7, Topic A, p 4	A-2
Editing macros using the Visual Basic Editor	Advanced	Unit 7, Topic B, p 10	B-2
Running macros	Advanced	Unit 7, Topic A, p 2	A-1
Modifying default font settings	Intermediate	Unit 3, Topic A, p 5	A-2
Setting the default number of worksheets	Intermediate	Unit 3, Topic A, p 5	
Changing the default file location for templates	Intermediate	Unit 8, Topic B, p 10	B-3

Course summary

This summary contains information to help you bring the course to a successful conclusion. Using this information, you will be able to:

A Use the summary text to reinforce what you've learned in class.

B Determine the next courses in this series (if any), as well as any other resources that might help you continue to learn about Excel 2003.

Topic A: Course summary

Use the following summary text to reinforce what you've learned in class.

Unit summaries

Unit 1

In this unit, you learned how to **zoom in** and **zoom out** on a **large worksheet** to view more or less of the data. Next, you learned how to **freeze** and **split panes** as well as how to **hide** and **unhide rows and columns** to view data more effectively. You also learned how to create an **outline** to summarize data by levels. Finally, you learned how to set **print titles** and **page breaks**, and you used the **Page Break Preview** feature to view and adjust page breaks.

Unit 2

In this unit, you learned how to **navigate** between multiple worksheets, name worksheets, and add color to worksheet tabs. You also learned how to **insert**, **rename**, **move**, **copy**, and **delete** worksheets, as well as how to **preview** and **print** multiple worksheets. Then, you learned how to create **3-D formulas** to perform calculations based on data from multiple worksheets, and you learned how to add a **Watch window** to a cell. Next, you learned how to summarize data by using the **Consolidate command**. Then, you created **links** to data in a different workbook, and you saw that Excel automatically updates data in the destination workbook when you change the data in the source workbook. Finally, you learned how to **redirect links**.

Unit 3

In this unit, you learned how to change the **View**, **General**, and **Calculation** settings of Excel by using the **Options dialog box**. You also learned how to **show**, **hide**, **move**, and **dock** toolbars, as well as how to **customize toolbars** and **menus** by adding and deleting buttons. Finally, you learned about **short menus.**

Unit 4

In this unit, you learned how to add **borders** and **shading** to a cell or a range by using the **Borders palette** and the **Fill Color palette**. Next, you learned how to apply **special number formats** to ZIP codes, Social Security numbers, and phone numbers, and you learned how to control the display of zero values. Then, you learned how to apply **date and time formats** and how to perform calculations on dates. You observed Excel's **built-in styles** and learned how to **create**, **modify**, and **apply styles**. Finally, you learned how to **merge** cells, change **cell orientation**, and **split** merged cells.

Unit 5

In this unit, you learned that a **list** is made up of **field names**, **fields**, and **records**. You learned how to **sort** a list by the information in one or more of its columns. You also learned how to use the **AutoFilter** command to display only rows that meet certain criteria. Next, you learned how to use the **Custom AutoFilter** dialog box to specify multiple conditions, using **comparison criteria** and **comparison operators**. Then, you created a **criteria range** to specify complex search conditions based on multiple column headings. Finally, you learned how to **copy filtered data** to a new location.

Unit 6

In this unit, you learned how to adjust the **scale** of a chart. You learned how to **format data points** and **explode slices** in a **pie chart** to highlight data. Then, you learned how to create a **combination chart** using two value axes. You also learned how to add a **trendline** to a chart. Next, you learned how to add, format, and move **graphic elements** in a chart. Finally, you learned how to **insert a picture** in a worksheet.

Unit 7

In this unit, you learned how to use trace **precedent cells** and **dependent cells** and how to **trace errors** by using the **Formula Auditing** toolbar. Next, you learned how to use **comments** and **text boxes** to add information to worksheets. Finally, you learned how to **protect** a worksheet to prevent unauthorized users from making changes.

Unit 8

In this unit, you used Excel's **built-in templates** to maintain sales invoices and expense statements. Then, you learned how to **create custom templates** containing any formatting, styles, content, and functionality you want. Finally, you learned how to **modify templates**.

Topic B: Continued learning after class

It is impossible to learn to use any software effectively in a single day. To get the most out of this class, you should begin working with Excel 2003 to perform real tasks as soon as possible. Course Technology also offers resources for continued learning.

Next courses in this series

This is the second course in this series. The next courses in this series are:

- *Excel 2003: Advanced*
- *Excel 2003: Power User*
- *Excel 2003: VBA Programming*

Other resources

For more information, visit www.course.com.

Excel 2003: Intermediate

Quick reference

Button	Shortcut keys	Function
		Displays a preview of the sheets to be printed.
		Expands a specific dialog box.
	CTRL + P	Prints a specific worksheet.
		Collapses a specific dialog box.
		Merges the cells in a column or a row and centers the text.
B	CTRL + B	Makes text bold.
A↓Z		Sorts a list in ascending order.
	CTRL + 1	Opens the dialog box of the selected chart element.
		Draws a text box in a worksheet, chart, or picture.
		Draws an arrow in a worksheet, chart, or picture.
		Shows or hides all the comments in a worksheet.
		Inserts new comments in a worksheet.

Button	Shortcut keys	Function
		Draws a tracer arrow from the active cell containing an error value to the cell that causes the error.
		Removes all tracer arrows from a worksheet.
		Traces the precedent cells of a selected cell.
		Traces the dependent cells of a selected cell.
		Scrolls through Tabs to show the Sheet tabs that are not visible.

Glossary

3-D Formula

A formula that refers to the same cell or range in multiple worksheets.

Calculation

The process of computing and displaying the results of formulas.

Cell Orientation

Refers to the direction of text flow in a cell.

Combination Chart

Includes two or more graph types in a single chart.

Conditional Formatting

Formatting that is applied to data only if a specific criteria is satisfied.

Criteria Range

A group of cells that contain a set of search conditions.

Dependent Cell

Relies on the value of another cell.

Destination Workbook

A workbook that contains a formula with an external reference.

Digital Certificate

An attachment that guarantees security for a file.

Digital Signature

An electronic security stamp that is used to authenticate files that are sent through the Internet.

Docked

A toolbar state used to describe when a toolbar is attached to an edge of the program window.

External Link

That part of a formula in one workbook that refers to a cell, range, or name in another workbook. Also called an external reference.

External Reference

That part of a formula in one workbook that refers to a cell, range, or name in another workbook. Also called an external link.

Field

A column of data in a list.

Field Name

A column heading, which appears in the first row of a list.

Floating

A toolbar state used to describe when a toolbar appears to hover over the worksheet.

Freeze Panes

A command that locks row or column headings in place so that when you scroll, these headings will remain visible.

Leader Line

Used in a chart to connect a data label to its associated data point.

List

A series of rows containing related data.

Outline

Organizes worksheet by grouping it in levels of detail.

Precedent Cell

Provides data to a specific cell.

Print Title

Text that you want to print as a heading on all pages.

Record

A row of data in a list.

Short Menu

A menu that doesn't display all available commands when you first open it.

Sizing Handles

Appear as small squares or circles around the border of a selected picture and are used to change its height and width.

Smart Menu

A menu that displays the commands that you use most frequently.

Sorting

Organizing the data in a list in ascending or descending order by the contents of one or more columns in the list.

Source Workbook

The workbook to which an external reference refers.

Splitting

Dividing a worksheet into panes so that you can see different areas simultaneously.

Style

A collection of formats that are saved and applied as a group.

Template

A workbook with predefined settings on which you can base new workbooks.

Trendline

A graphical representation of drifts or variations in a data series.

Watch Window

A dialog box that displays values and formulas in another linked worksheet without navigating there.

Workspace

A logical container of related workbooks that retains page setups, window sizes, and display settings.

Index